SCHOLASTIC

GRADES
5 & UP

50 COMMON CORE READING RESPONSE ACTIVITIES

MARILYN PRYLE

New York • Toronto • London • Auckland • Sydney
New Delhi • Mexico City • Hong Kong • Buenos Aires

Teaching Resources

DEDICATION

Since this book was born out of a question a bright and curious student observer asked me, I dedicate it to all new teachers: May you reap the deep rewards of this profession as you guide children to a better understanding of our world and themselves. May you be strong and always optimistic. May you never stop questioning.

ACKNOWLEDGMENTS

I am profoundly grateful for the support of many people. I am first and foremost grateful to all the students who have passed through my classroom over the last few years and patiently endured my ideas, some of which worked, and some of which didn't. I also thank the community and administration of the Abington Heights School District for their continued support of my work. Of course, this book is a result of the encouragement, vision, and expertise of many people at Scholastic, including Virginia Dooley, Joanna Davis-Swing, and Sarah Glasscock, and I am truly grateful to them. Lastly, anything positive I have achieved in this life is because of the support and love given to me by my family: Ernest and Patricia Bogusch, Bill and Rosemarie Pryle, my husband Tim, and my patient, smart, joyful boys Tiernan and Gavin.

Cover design: Jorge J. Namerow

Interior photographs: Marilyn Pryle

Interior design: Melinda Belter

Development Editor: Joanna Davis-Swing

Editor: Sarah Glasscock

Copy Editor: David Klein

ISBN: 978-0-545-62677-4

Copyright © 2014 by Marilyn Pryle

All rights reserved.

Printed in the U.S.A.

1 2 3 4 5 6 7 8 9 10   40   21 20 19 18 17 16 15 14

TABLE OF CONTENTS

Introduction

When Pennsylvania officially adopted the Common Core State Standards (CCSS), my district, like others, moved quickly to make sure all personnel knew, understood, and implemented them. At the first English department meeting about it, most teachers, myself included, picked up the photocopy of the CCSS with a resigned commitment—we would do whatever it asked, but we had been through this before. Someone even said, "Here we go again!" We knew what we were doing; we were passionate readers and thinkers ourselves, and we knew how to teach English; we had been trained and retrained. Everyone was open to improvement, but how many more times would we be asked to shift our focus in a new way?

As I flipped through the pages of the CCSS, however, I began to think, *This is different.* These standards seemed simpler than past standards, and the ideas made more sense. They seemed to focus on the basics of good reading and writing, and yet also seemed realistically challenging in what they expected kids to do at each grade. They seemed open-ended—I realized that any number of lessons or teaching styles could help meet the CCSS requirements. In fact, I realized that much of what my colleagues and I were already doing supported the CCSS. The document turned out to be a validation of our efforts, not a condemnation of them. What a relief!

At the same time, I could see that the rigor of the CCSS would require me to push students a bit more—not by cramming in more material, but by going more deeply into what we were reading. Instead of focusing primarily on characters, plot, and theme, I would have to teach students how to thoroughly unpack a text and ask themselves what the author was trying to do and why. I would have to get them to think like critics and not just students. They would no longer simply be extracting information and lessons from a text; they would be figuring out how a text works.

To be sure, I had done this somewhat in the past. But to see the CCSS emphasize it so strongly made me realize that I had been underestimating students. They were capable, even in middle school, of not just comprehending a text but also of analyzing its craft and structure, and placing it in the overall scope of texts they had read. It's not that I hadn't taught these things; it was more that they had been an afterthought, a side note to plot and theme. I realized that I had to make the bigger picture—the author's purpose and choices, and the text's place among other literature—more of a priority. The future of English education would no longer be about ensuring memorization of characters and plots, but about ensuring that all students could approach any text, ask deeper questions of it, and answer those questions.

The emphasis of the CCSS, then, is on process, on acquiring the skills of close, careful readers. The standards are about quality, not quantity. They focus on depth, not surface gimmicks. Students can acquire skills not by any new "quick fixes" but only by the constant practice of reading a variety of texts in an in-depth way. As an experienced English teacher and a close, careful reader who enjoys thinking about craft and how a text fits with others I've read, I feel more confident than ever. So often, new governmental requirements make teachers feel discouraged and inadequate, but I don't think this is the case with the Common

50 Common Core Reading Response Activities © 2014 by Marilyn Pryle, Scholastic Teaching Resources

Core. After reading the CCSS many times, I've had three consistent thoughts:

- *This is, in fact, how good readers read.*
- *Yes, I've been an effective teacher so far.*
- *I can push students even further, in a way that will benefit them as readers, scholars, and thinkers.*

The purpose of this book is to help other teachers who may feel overwhelmed by, nervous about, or simply unsure about the Common Core State Standards. The lessons presented here are fun, easy, common-sense ideas that will help students interact with texts in a meaningful way. Some are old and time-tested; some have been created more recently with the Common Core in mind. Don't feel that you must do each lesson with everything you read—these lessons and practices overlap in skill and focus, and are meant to provide a variety of approaches throughout the year. Please pick and choose, alter, skip, add, and rewrite them in any way that seems helpful to you and your students. We must continue to believe that our instincts, not only as educators but also as readers and lovers of texts, are accurate, well informed, and beneficial to students and other teachers.

How to Use This Book

I have divided the book into two parts. You can, and should, tweak or rework the ideas in both sections to most effectively accommodate your students. Although these ideas have worked for me, you are the expert in your classroom.

PART 1: Practices: This section includes ideas to incorporate daily, or on an ongoing basis. These are some of the most effective steps you can take as a teacher; it is by constant practice that we become experts at anything. Through this practice, students can fully internalize certain concepts and deep-reading habits, such as close reading analysis, genre identification, and an understanding of figurative language and poetic technique.

PART 2: Individual Activities: This section offers activities to apply to many different texts. Use whichever one fits your current text and class needs best.

Lesson Overview: Each lesson contains the following components:

- *A CC Connection! box like the one below*
- *A list of the materials you'll need*
- *A brief explanation of the lesson's benefits*
- *Instructions for carrying out the lesson*

> ## CC CONNECTION!
>
> Each lesson is directly linked to a standard in the CCSS "College and Career Readiness Anchor Standards for Reading" for Grades 6–12. For simplicity's sake, I use these general Anchor Standards instead of the ELA grade-specific set of standards.

Assessing Students' Work: Some lessons contain a "Build a Rubric" box with suggestions about how to customize your assessment to fit your students' needs. Lessons that do not have an assessment suggestion can be graded with a class participation grade, or not numerically graded at all.

I sincerely hope the ideas here help you and your students. Enjoy!

Easy Reading Responses

What It Is: A short written response to a text that includes a citation

Use It With: Fiction and nonfiction

Doing Reading Responses (RRs) is one of the most effective techniques I know for getting kids to refer to the text. It is also a method of discussion in upper-level high school classes and college seminars: Students lead a discussion of their assigned reading, offering their thoughts and questions while referencing page numbers, paragraphs, and sentences. The teacher merely facilitates, filling in information or deepening questions as needed. This type of student-driven discussion can also be an invaluable experience for middle-school students: It helps them cultivate the habit of being active readers, thinking and responding to a text as they read, and formulating cohesive thoughts directly tied to it.

MATERIALS

✓ Reading Response (RR) Guidelines for each student, p. 9
Note: Students store these guidelines in their binders because they will refer to them all year. With consistent practice, students will soon have these guidelines memorized, but encourage them to reread the guidelines periodically to challenge themselves by choosing different RRs.

✓ Assignment: Reading Response (RR) Analysis Paper for each student, p. 11

✓ Sticky notes

✓ Students' collection of Reading Response entries

✓ 11-inch x 14-inch sheet of paper for each student (optional)

CC CONNECTION!

To complete a Reading Response, students must:

• "read closely" and "cite specific textual evidence . . . to support conclusions" (R.1) • depending on which Reading Response they choose, "determine . . . themes" (R.2) or examine the development of characters or events (R.3).

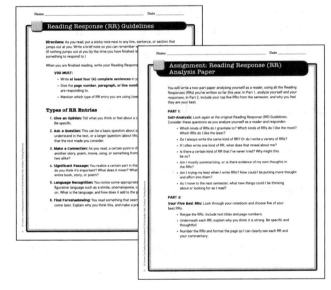

DIRECTIONS

* Hand out the Reading Response (RR) Guidelines to students and discuss them: what each RR involves; which responses are best for fiction, which are best for nonfiction, and which could be used for both; and so on. (At the beginning of the year, I have students write RRs in class.)

* Students read the assigned text in class or for homework. They place a sticky note next to any line, sentence, or paragraph that jumps out at them. To remember what they

were thinking, students write a brief note to themselves on the sticky note. If nothing jumps out, they should reread the text to find something to respond to.

* After completing the reading, students use their notes to write an RR.

One of my steadfast rules is that students write a minimum of four complete sentences. I want students to push themselves to think through to the next thought, one that might never have surfaced were it not nudged forth. If students can elaborate, explain, or round out the original idea just a bit further, they will not only learn something but also develop their ability and the habit to do so in the future. (And based on my experience as a holistic scorer of standardized essays, I can definitely say that student writers who take their ideas deeper—without repeating them—are the ones who receive the higher scores on their papers.)

On an Ask a Question RR, for example, students can set up a question and then write three sentences about what they understand so far, ask a question and then think of three more, or ask a question and speculate on possible answers.

Favorite Tweet!

Kelly Gallagher: "It doesn't matter how good the writing standards are if students aren't writing way more than the teacher can read" (2013).

Assessing the Work: I rarely collect RRs. Instead, on days on which they are due, I give students another activity to work on, and I circulate to check that the RRs have been done. Sometimes, I just skim the RRs and comment or ask a question; if time permits, I ask each student to summarize the RR for me. I love this method because it enables me

to have a 60-second reading conference with each student. I check whether the RR is labeled logically: the goal of the practice is first to get students to meaningfully and specifically respond to a text, and second to have them consciously realize they are doing so (via labeling). As long as students can see that they are deliberate literary critics, any logical link to one of the RR types will do. I can give a grade on the spot for the criteria listed on the Reading Response (RR) Guidelines, usually a score of 0–4.

Quizzes: On quizzes, I often include a prompt like, "Read through your RRs and rewrite the best one below. Then tell why you think it is one of your best." This direction not only sends students back to the material, but it also makes them reflect on their own process of responding.

Sharing the Work: I usually have students share their RRs with a partner or small group. Sometimes, I have each group choose the best one or two RRs to read to the entire class. Other times, I ask the class if anyone would like to share an RR. Again, through these methods, the main ideas of the reading are usually revealed—not by me, but by the students themselves.

A Step Further: Post the RRs

Besides having students discuss their RRs in a small-group or whole-class setting, I sometimes have them share RRs in writing. Students write a summary of their RR (one or two sentences) with a quote from the book, if applicable, on a sheet of 11-x-14-inch paper. After taping their work at eye-level in the classroom, they read as many of their classmates' RRs as they can and write a response on each sheet. Students must

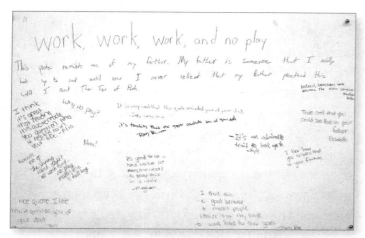

A reader's response to the phrase "work, work, work, and no play" and the responses of classmates

write something meaningful—an opinion, connection, or question. This gets them moving, reading, and thinking.

Students can also share and respond to RRs online, via a blog or Web site like Edmodo (https://www.edmodo.com). They can type in their RRs and post meaningful replies below each classmate's entry. Sometimes, the discussion in writing goes deeper than in the face-to-face class discussion!

> I put in RRs evidence of my thoughts to show that I understand the readings. From my evidence, I can connect to the readings better and have a better grasp of the books.
> —*James*

Another Step Further: The Reading Response Analysis Paper

At the end of a quarter or semester, I assign a two-part Reading Response Analysis Paper. Students read through all their RRs and analyze their reading and thinking habits. This is an invaluable step; the practice of not only processing the text but of also dissecting

one's own habits will benefit students for years to come.

Part 1: Self-Analysis: Students reflect on which RRs they gravitate to, which seem difficult to use, and which they have never tried. They ask if they are writing RRs to the best of their ability and if, in the future, they could try harder. They commit to trying RRs they have not thus far attempted. Regardless of the actual future outcome, students benefit from looking over their working and thinking processes.

> RRs have helped me become better at English and writing assignments . . . I try to find a deeper meaning in the stories.
> —*Brendan*

Part 2: Five Best RRs: Students choose their five best RRs. They type out the RRs and write a sentence or two about why they think each RR is effective. This compels them to focus on what they already have done well; my hope is that it will motivate them to continue to build off those skills.

If you give any kind of quarterly or semester test, you will find that the Reading Response Analysis Paper can serve as an effective review: In choosing their five best RRs, students must read through all the RRs from the quarter or semester, thus bringing to mind plotlines, themes, and characters. My students usually enjoy writing these papers, and I enjoy reading them. It's always gratifying to hear students evaluate their own progress and direct their own future growth.

> The more we do them, the more I think they are important for the future and it forces me to read the story even though I may not like it.
> —*Dani*

Reading Response (RR) Guidelines

Directions: As you read, put a sticky note next to any line, sentence, or section that jumps out at you. Write a brief note so you can remember what you were thinking. (If nothing jumps out at you by the time you have finished reading, go back and **FIND** something to respond to.)

When you are finished reading, write your Reading Response on a sheet of paper.

YOU MUST:

- Write **at least four (4) complete sentences** in your RR.
- Give the **page number**, **paragraph, or line number** of the part you are responding to.
- Mention which type of RR entry you are using (see below).

Types of RR Entries

1. **Give an Opinion:** Tell what you think or feel about a certain part, and why. Be specific.

2. **Ask a Question:** This can be a basic question about something you don't understand in the text, or a larger question (about life, literature, or anything) that the text made you consider.

3. **Make a Connection:** As you read, a certain point in the text reminds you of another story, poem, movie, song, or something from real life. How are the two alike?

4. **Significant Passage:** You realize a certain part in the text is important. Why do you think it's important? What does it mean? What does it tell you about the entire book, story, or poem?

5. **Language Recognition:** You notice some appropriate sensory details, or figurative language such as a simile, onomatopoeia, or personification, and so on. What is the language, and how does it add to the piece?

6. **Find Foreshadowing:** You read something that seems like a hint of what will come later. Explain why you think this, and make a prediction.

50 Common Core Reading Response Activities © 2014 by Marilyn Pryle, Scholastic Teaching Resources

Reading Response (RR) Guidelines

7. **Theme Recognition:** You find a sentence or two that might be the theme (the "So what?") of the piece. Explain it in your own words.

8. **Spot the Setting:** You notice a part that refers to the place or time of the story or poem. Why is it important?

9. **Character Description:** You notice a detail about a character (what he or she looks like, thinks, says, or does). Why is it important? What does it reveal about that character?

10. **Mark the Motivation:** You realize a character's motive(s) (what a character wants). Explain the motive(s) and its effect on the story or other characters.

11. **Detect the Conflict:** You realize one of the conflicts or problems in the story. Explain it, and explain how you recognized it.

12. **Find the Climax:** You read a part that you realize is the biggest event (or most important moment) in the story. Explain **why** it is so important.

13. **Cite the Claim:** You find the sentence that is the author's main argument (the thesis or claim). Explain why you think it is the focus of the piece.

14. **Interesting Intro:** You think the author's introduction is interesting, clever, or engaging. Tell what technique the author used and why you think it is effective.

15. **Clever Conclusion:** You think the author's conclusion or clincher is really effective. Tell what technique the author used and why it works.

Assignment: Reading Response (RR) Analysis Paper

You will write a two-part paper analyzing yourself as a reader, using all the Reading Responses (RRs) you've written so far this year. In Part 1, analyze yourself and your responses. In Part 2, include your top five RRs from the semester, and why you feel they are your best.

PART 1:

Self-Analysis: Look again at the original Reading Response (RR) Guidelines. Consider these questions as you analyze yourself as a reader and responder:

- Which kinds of RRs do I gravitate to? Which kinds of RRs do I like the most? Which RRs do I like the least?

- Do I always write the same kind of RR? Or do I write a variety of RRs?

- If I often write one kind of RR, what does that reveal about me?

- Is there a certain kind of RR that I've never tried? Why might this be so?

- Am I mostly summarizing, or is there evidence of my own thoughts in the RRs?

- Am I trying my best when I write RRs? How could I be putting more thought and effort into them?

- As I move to the next semester, what new things could I be thinking about or looking for as I read?

PART 2:

Your Five Best RRs: Look through your notebook and choose five of your best RRs.

- Retype the RRs. Include text titles and page numbers.

- Underneath each RR, explain why you think it is strong. Be specific and thoughtful!

- Number the RRs and format the page so I can clearly see each RR and your commentary.

50 Common Core Reading Response Activities © 2014 by Marilyn Pryle, Scholastic Teaching Resources

A Poem a Day

What It Is: Class time to expose students to poetry in general and poetic techniques and styles

Use It With: Poetry

What I love about this method is that every student can contribute once he or she is familiar with some of the basics of poetry. I never want any student to feel like he just "doesn't get it" or that she's not "deep enough." Poetry is part of us all, and even kids who can't immediately access the theme of the day's poem can participate in identifying a simile, some alliteration, or the meter of the first stanza.

MATERIALS

✓ a copy of the poems for each student (I can usually copy the entire week's poems on a single page.)

DIRECTIONS

* Hand out copies of the poem(s) at the beginning of class.

* Give students a few minutes to silently read and annotate the day's poem.

* Ask open-ended questions. Start with, "What do you see here?"

* Let students direct the discussion. Wait for them to identify whatever they wish, whether it be some technical aspect, the theme, a twist of language, or a connection to another work. For example, a student might say, "I don't know what this poem is about, but there's a simile in the second stanza." "Excellent!" I respond, and we go from there. If the class stalls out at some point without reaching the heart of the poem, I direct them with questions like, "What do you think the author means in line five?" or "What's the feeling you get

CC CONNECTION!

Discussing a poem a day requires students to:

• "read closely . . . and make logical inferences" and "cite specific textual evidence" (R.1)

• determine central ideas (R.2)

• determine "connotative and figurative meanings," and "analyze word choices" (R.4)

• question structure, point of view, and author's purpose (R.5, R.6)

when you read a phrase like 'dark, misty field'?" and in this way, try to guide them to the main meaning of the poem. Usually, however, they get there on their own.

Sharing a poem a day requires some commitment, but you can quickly and easily manage this with these shortcuts:

Use short poems: This will save on time and photocopying.

Use accessible poems, at least in the beginning: Choose poems that can be easily understood, so students don't get discouraged. Reassure them often that poems are not meant to be "unlocked" like some secret code—poems are meant to be explored over a lifetime. I tell students that I rarely understand any poem when I first read it and that I must reread it several times to get even a basic understanding of it.

Do fewer poems: If you are overwhelmed or simply don't have the time, do a poem every other day, or twice a week. Even doing a poem once a week can help students immensely! Just be sure to stick to the schedule you choose, so students know when to settle into "poetry mode."

50 Common Core Reading Response Activities © 2014 by Marilyn Pryle, Scholastic Teaching Resources

Focus on only one or two main points within each poem: Fully explicating a poem could take a whole class or two—and that's not the idea with this practice. In the beginning, focus on teaching only one easy concept per poem, like alliteration, assonance, onomatopoeia, simile, metaphor, or imagery. After you teach a concept, you can refer to it in the future, but don't try to teach all the aspects of each poem every day.

Tip: If a discussion about a poem could go longer, return to it the next day instead of introducing a new poem.

A Step Further: Link Form and Content

Poets deliberately select the techniques they employ, including rhyme, meter, alliteration, and similes, to enhance the content. Linking form and content is a sophisticated concept, but one that students can easily understand—and enjoy—with a bit of practice. The habit of questioning form and content will be helpful to kids not just with poetry but with other genres as well. I want students to try to think like authors, and ask themselves questions like, *Why free verse here? Why this rhyme scheme? Why this letter for alliteration? Why this meter? Why this specific metaphor?* I want them to get in the habit of discovering the author's purpose, a major tenet of the CCSS and a repeated theme on standardized tests.

The trick is to question students in a way that leads them to the answer, at least in the beginning. If students start to feel "dumb" in front of a poem (instead of curious or investigative), the whole poem-a-day philosophy is lost. Here are some examples of how to guide students toward finding meaning in a poem:

"Like Ghosts of Eagles" by Robert Francis (1974): *Why is the "s" sound a good one to alliterate in a poem about rivers?*

"We Real Cool" by Gwendolyn Brooks (2005) or "Nothing Gold Can Stay" by Robert Frost (1995): *Why is the syllable count cut short in the last line?* (Both poems are about situations or lives that are cut short.)

"Bereft" by Robert Frost (1995): *Why would a poem about not letting go of a lost loved one have a rhyme scheme where the "A" rhyme continues for five lines and then reappears in line eight?*

"Secret Heart" by Robert P. Tristram Coffin (n.d.): *Why is this poem about a father and son written in couplets?*

"Woman With Flower" by Naomi Long Madgett (1970): *Why would a poem about letting flowers (and people) grow up on their own instead of smothering them be written in free verse?*

"Poem" by William Carlos Williams (1986): *How do these lines mimic a cat carefully stepping?*

Once, while the class was analyzing Walt Whitman's "When I Heard the Learn'd Astronomer," a student said, "Oh, I get it—the repetition of 'When' in the first half shows how boring the lecture was—like it was just a bunch of repeating." Though I'd noticed the repetition in earlier readings, I had honestly never made that connection before.

A wonderful transformation that begins to happen once kids start to inquisitively examine form is that they often point out connections I had never noticed myself! On the next page are some poems I've used in the past, arranged by a dominant (but not the only) literary technique.

Alliteration

"All But Blind," Walter de la Mare

"The Sidewalk Racer," Lillian Morrison

"Preludes," T. S. Eliot

"Earth," Oliver Herford

Assonance

"Stories," J. Patrick Lewis

"Seashells," Douglas Florian

Free Verse

"The Hawk," Mary Oliver

"Gift," Czeslaw Milosz

"Dog on a Chain," Charles Simic

"Sisters," Lucille Clifton

"The Universe," May Swenson

Internal Rhyme

"Summer Stars," Carl Sandburg

"Mean Song," Eve Merriam

"Snow Toward Evening," Melville Cane

Onomatopoeia

"Sonic Boom," John Updike

"Onomatopoeia," Eve Merriam

"Fall Wind," Aileen Fisher

Personification

"The Waking," Theodore Roethke

"Waiting for the Storm," Timothy Steele

"Night," Francis William Bourdillon

"Fog," Carl Sandburg

"The Breathing," Denise Levertov

Repetition

"When I Heard the Learn'd Astronomer," Walt Whitman

"The Raven," Edgar Allan Poe

"The Pasture," Robert Frost

"The Child on the Shore," Ursula K. LeGuin

"Stopping by Woods on a Snowy Evening," Robert Frost

Simile or Metaphor

"Youth," Langston Hughes

"Steam Shovel," Charles Malam

"The Sea," James Reeves

"Metaphor," Eve Merriam

"Dreams," Langston Hughes

With consistent practice, students will become comfortable and adept at recognizing several literary devices; they also will develop a deeper understanding of form. All these skills will serve them on standardized tests. More important, though, these skills, and the poems they are packaged in, will enhance students' lives, since any time spent with good poetry is time spent with the deeper truths of this world. The ability to approach a poem is one of the greatest gifts we as English teachers can provide our students.

50 Common Core Reading Response Activities © 2014 by Marilyn Pryle, Scholastic Teaching Resources

Analyze Art

What It Is: Class time for students to discuss a work of art

Use It With: Any genre, fiction or nonfiction, to make connections and practice evidence-based close-looking skills

I didn't realize the deep benefits of using art in class until I attended an inspiring conference session led by professionals from the Smithsonian American Art Museum. After hearing these curator-educators, I vowed to more regularly seek out art I could use in my classes.

A few simple questions are all you need to facilitate a lively discussion of art and to foster deep critical-thinking skills. Discussing art—alone or with a text—not only engages students, but it also reinforces the skills they need for effective reading. Showing students works of art and having them name, interpret, draw conclusions about, and evaluate what they see can help them become better readers.

MATERIALS

✓ Any work of art: a painting, photograph, or sculpture (display copy and a copy for each student)

> ### Laser Power!
> Students love coming up to the screen to point out what they see. Mine also love using the laser pointer on my PowerPoint remote!

DIRECTIONS

* Display the work of art and distribute copies. The piece could relate to your text in some way (as an actual illustration or a representative image of the era).

* Discuss the art with the whole class, or have pairs or small groups write their answers to the following questions first: "What do

> ### CC CONNECTION!
> By analyzing a picture, students practice close looking, making logical inferences, and determining central ideas (R.1, R.2).

you notice?" and "What else do you notice?" That's it! The key, however, which I did not learn until later, is not to stop after the first few responses and then explain everything yourself. Push students to look more deeply at the picture by asking questions like "What could that mean?" and "Why?" When you feel like the discussion has exhausted itself (or time is running short), try a question about the art's overall meaning, message, or effect. If the art relates to a text, ask guiding questions that might help students understand the art and how it relates to the text. Spend the most time, though, just asking kids what they see.

Tip: Don't correct students' observations or interpretations. Let them think and speak freely—as long as they can point to something in the picture as support.

Here's a sample discussion of "The Great Wave off Kanagawa" by Hokusai:

Ms. P.: Take time to look at this print. (*I wait a few minutes.*) What do you see?

Kerrie: A tidal wave.

Aimee: Like it has claws.

Ms. P.: Good. What else?

Jeremy: Writing. Maybe it's Chinese?

Ms. P.: Good. What else?

Chris: It's winter.

Ms. P.: What makes you say that?

Chris: There are snowflakes around the wave.

Mark: That's just water splashing.

(*Some students seem surprised by this.*)

Ms. P.: What does everyone think: snowflakes or splash? (*We decide it's water splashing.*) Good. What else? (*After the first "wave" of answers, it usually takes longer for students to respond.*)

Jeremy: Is that a wave in the very back?

Noah: I thought it was a mountain.

Ms. P.: What makes you say that?

Noah: It has a peak. It's in the distance. It doesn't look like a claw like the other waves do.

Ms. P.: Great details! What do you think the white part is on it?

Noah: I guess . . . snow?

Chris: So there *is* snow!

Ms. P.: The background might show a snow-covered mountain. It looks like it has a peak, as Noah said. What else?

Aimee: It could be a volcano—the peak looks jagged at the top.

Ms. P.: Excellent detail, Aimee!

Drew: Is that a boat?!

Ms. P.: Where do you see one?

Drew: (*pointing*) Right there, that thin, yellow thing . . . and there are people in it!

Kerrie: They look scared.

Ms. P.: Why?

Kerrie: They're crouching.

Drew: And there's another boat, behind it!

(*We continue until responses fade. I end with these questions.*)

Ms. P.: In this picture, what's big and what's small?

Hannah: The wave is big. The volcano is small.

Ms. P.: What's smaller than the volcano?

Hannah: The drops? No—the men in the boat.

Ms. P.: Yes! Do you see that? What do you think the artist is saying here?

Richie: Nature is more important than people?

Ms. P.: Nature is certainly bigger than people, right? But are people left out of the picture? (*Students shake their heads.*) Right—they are in the picture. Are humans separate from nature?

Chris: They're in the boat, but waves surround them. They're kind of mixed in with nature.

Ms. P.: So humans *are* a part of nature, but a big or small part? Someone put it all together.

Aimee: Humans are a part of nature, but a small part.

Ms. P.: Excellent. What do you think the title of this is?

Kim: "The Killer Wave."

Noah: "The Volcano Waits."

Drew: "Don't Take Your Boat Out in a Storm."

After a few more guesses, I reveal the title. As we examine haikus and tankas, forms of Japanese poetry, I direct students to recall the art and their interpretations of its meaning. Since the woodcut is a visual text, and we have discussed it deeply, students will remember it, possibly more than the poems!

A Step Further: Transfer to Text

During reading, ask: *What do you notice? What else? What could this mean? Why?* Every detail an author includes about characters, setting, and plot serves a purpose. When students are in the habit of noticing details, articulating them, making inferences about them, and evaluating them, they are becoming skillful and lifelong readers.

Quote Wall

What It Is: Wall space covered with quotes from your readings throughout the year, arranged by theme

Use It With: All genres—fiction, nonfiction, poetry, drama

MATERIALS
✓ Sheet of white paper and/or construction paper
✓ Tape
✓ Markers and decorative materials (optional)

Francis Bacon (1561–1626) reportedly kept a notebook arranged by theme—the pages had titles such as "Love," "Truth," and "Friendship." Bacon would jot down quotations that inspired him, along with the author's name, under the appropriate theme in the notebook. Before long, his notebook was filled with themes and quotations from a myriad of sources, and it became the basis for his famous work, *The Essays* (1999).

Wouldn't it be wonderful if, instead of passively reading, students not only sought out the deeper meanings in a text but also sought to make thematic connections among a variety of texts? If students learned to listen as texts speak not only to readers but also to *one another*? People who live rich reading lives know this. Designating a space in your classroom for a Quote Wall can help plant this seed.

DIRECTIONS
* Write words on paper that represent some of the themes addressed throughout your curriculum and attach it to the wall. You could display themes at the beginning of the year so students anticipate them, or wait until they read a text to post a theme.

* Throughout the year, encourage students to find sentences in their reading that connect to themes on the Quote Wall. You could make this an extra-credit task, or have students take turns finding quotes all year. This could also be a partner activity at certain points in the year. When they find a quote, students should write or type it on a piece of paper, including a citation (speaker/author, title, page number). Once you approve (and proofread!) a quote, the student can enlarge, color, decorate, or otherwise arrange it to become wall-worthy.

By the end of the year, you'll have quotes from various sources (and hopefully from several genres) about each theme, and students can draw parallels or compare and contrast them. You can have many fruitful discussions about the nuances within each theme, the perceptions of the speakers/authors of the quotes, and the role of the genre in dealing with themes.

Real-Life Connection: Strategically Place Themes: The theme of "Being Open to New Experiences" could hang outside your door, so students see it as they enter your room. A theme like "Facing Challenges" could be posted near the gym; "Having Perspective" could be displayed around windows; "Taking Responsibility" could be effective in a disciplinary area. This won't work for every theme, of course, but one or two appropriately placed themes might help students see how literature connects to our real lives.

Cross-Curricular Idea!: Teachers in other subject areas can also create their own Quote Walls centered around themes, and you can overlap themes and combine students' quotes. For example, a theme like "Survival" could include quotes from fiction and poetry students read in English class, and from letters or biographies they read in social studies class. An ELA teacher and a science teacher could collaborate on a theme like "Life Cycles." This is a wonderful way to encourage students to think broadly about our world, to search for connections beyond the four walls of English class! Different subjects could even be color-coded on the Quote Wall to more dramatically demonstrate the integration of curricula.

Variation

Quote Anthology: Instead of setting up a Quote Wall, you could have students, like Bacon, keep a notebook to the same effect. (You could even do both the wall *and* notebook!) Students begin a notebook page for the themes they encounter in their reading, leaving two to three pages in between each one for adding quotations as the year progresses.

I also suggest having students set up a running table of contents at the beginning of the notebook so they can easily locate themes. By the end of the year, students will have an exciting collection of the most significant passages from their readings to take with them into the future.

It's Contagious!
You might have students come to you with ideas for themes. As long as they have quotes to support the theme, make room on the wall for it.

A Step Further: The Personal Essay

Once the Quote Wall and/or Quote Anthology is filling up, students could, again like Bacon, write short essays on the themes. Bacon titled his essays with the themes themselves: "On Trust," "On Friendship," "On Love," and so on. He would develop his own thesis on a theme and explore it using his quotes combined with personal experience. Ask students to do the same: Choose a theme that speaks to them, craft a claim, and write an essay using relevant quotes, personal experience, and any other appropriate sources (films or songs, for example) that support their thesis.

50 Common Core Reading Response Activities © 2014 by Marilyn Pryle, Scholastic Teaching Resources

Poetry Modeling

What It Is: Students write their own poems in the form or style of an existing poem.

Use It With: Poetry

Whenever possible, have students write poems —not just acrostics, but real, meaty poems that employ the techniques you present in class. This can be difficult to do from scratch; instead, help students craft poems directly scaffolded from the ones they have read.

MATERIALS

✓ a copy of a poem you've taught in class for each student

DIRECTIONS

There are a few ways students can model a poem they've read and studied. Present only one of these at a time, or let students choose one once they're familiar with the method.

Have students write poems modeling the content of the original poem. If the poem has a strong central theme or idea, ask students to write poems repeating the theme but using another image. The slide below gives directions for using the poem "Elephant in the Dark" by Jalal ad Din Rumi (1995). The poem is a retelling of an ancient tale about five men who

each feel a different part of an elephant in the dark, and each guesses that the elephant is something else. (For example, the man who touches the elephant's leg thinks it is a column in a temple.) Rumi concludes that if everyone had gone in together with candles, they would have realized it was an elephant. This is a wonderful poem about the blessings and limits of each person's individual intelligence, and about the benefits of working together. Ask students to read aloud their poems without titles and let the rest of the class guess what is in the dark.

You could also remove the main "noun" of the poem and have students replace it and rewrite the poem.

Have students write poems modeling a dominant technique of the original poem. One such dominant technique I love to have students imitate is the extended metaphor, which can be found in poems such as Langston Hughes's "Mother to Son" (1995). Students should create a metaphor for something in their lives and then think of ways to extend the metaphor. See the slide on the next page for directions.

I have students write in free verse, but as you can see, I set a minimum line length and require three extensions of the metaphor (in the Hughes poem, for example, the main

> **Modeling Poetry: Write a poem modeled on "Elephant in the Dark"**
>
> - Choose an <u>animal</u> or <u>object</u> that 4–5 people will inspect in the dark.
> - Describe the mistakes each person makes.
> - Have a <u>stanza</u> for <u>each person</u>. Each stanza should be at least 3 lines.
> - As an ending for the poem, add one final stanza and put Rumi's final idea in your own words.
> - Title it "_____ in the Dark."

metaphor is the staircase and some of the "extensions" are the boards torn up, the bare spots, and the landings). This is a fun idea to do in pairs, and I always enjoy reading the poems they produce. If you have read a poem primarily for a central metaphor, a string of similes, or a symphony of onomatopoeia, you could have students try that technique as well.

Have students write poems modeling the structure of the original. This is the technique I employ when, for instance, students write haiku. They could imitate a rhyme scheme (though, as pointed out in the box to the right, writing quality poetry in a rhyme scheme is a challenge). Students could try a ballad, a tanka, or even a sonnet. The key to success with this option is to provide several examples of accessible poems in the structure

of the original poem, and to describe the purpose of the structure and why poets use it. For example, the haiku is not simply three lines of words broken into syllable counts of five-seven-five. It is structured to build a small world that ends with a surprise. The last line should be a twist in some way, a new perspective, a breaking open of thought. A sonnet, on the other hand, is built to be an argument with a turn midway and a conclusion. A ballad is constructed to hold a rolling story of any length. When students imitate structure, it should reflect their deep understanding of how form meets content.

However you choose to incorporate poetry modeling into your curriculum, it will have real benefits. Students will gain an inside perspective on how poets think and craft their work. By imitating the work of established poets, students learn techniques and forms and get to feel what it's like to transform profound ideas into words.

To Rhyme or Not to Rhyme?

Unless rhyming is dictated by the form of a poem, I discourage it. For middle school students, trying to find rhymes takes over the poem at the expense of every other poetic technique, and the final result often sounds silly or even nonsensical.

Genre Index

What It Is: A running list of all genres studied throughout the year

Use It With: Fiction, nonfiction, film, plays, art, infographics

Another yearlong practice that will help information sink in over the long term is having students keep a Genre Index. Each time the class reads or studies a text, whether print or nonprint and regardless of size, have students record its title and author and determine its genre. This quick and easy practice will go far in helping students understand audience, purpose, and tone.

MATERIALS

✓ Notebooks

✓ Every single print and nonprint text you study!

DIRECTIONS

* Tell students to reserve a few pages in their notebooks for the Genre Index. Work with them to create categories for "Title," "Author," and "Genre."

* Each time you read a text, have students record the pertinent information in the Genre Index. At the beginning of the reading, ask students to note only the title and author since they might not be able to determine the genre at first glance. Also, as they approach the text, they will be thinking, "What's the genre of this text?" That is a habit of good readers!

Don't Give Away the Genre!

Make students ask themselves, "What is this? What is this author trying to do? Why did this author write this?"

CC CONNECTION!

In order to name the genres of texts, students must "analyze the structure of texts" (R.5) and "assess how … purpose shapes the content and style of a text" (R.6).

So often we want to give as much information as possible before the class reads, so we introduce a text by saying, "Take a look at this persuasive essay from the editorial section of the paper" or "Here's a poem that relates to the novel we just finished." If, like me, you usually start a reading this way, try to catch yourself! Teaching students to figure out genre and purpose on their own is one of the most practical and lifelong skills we can impart. It will serve them long after they have passed standardized tests and finished school.

* Help students determine whatever information is available for nonprint texts. For example, if students watch a movie or play, the "author" may be the screenwriter or playwright. An infographic might not include the creator's name, but it might list the publishing company.

Tip: Introduce students to as many subgenres as possible and have them be specific about labeling the genre of a text. Every shade of a given genre that we can make visible to students will help them in determining an author's purpose. A list of several subgenres appears on the next page.

Fiction
Legend
Myth
Folk Tale
Short Story
Novella
Novel
Historical Fiction
Science Fiction
Children's Book

Poetry
Free Verse Poem
Ode
Ballad
Poetry Sequence
Rhyming Poem
Sonnet
Sestina
Villanelle

Essays
Descriptive
Autobiographical
Process
Classification
Setting Sketch
Character Sketch
Compare/Contrast
Persuasive
Analysis
Research
Reflection/Personal

Drama
One-Act Play
Play
Monologue
Soliloquy
Film
Television Show

Newspaper/ Journal Articles
News Account
Eyewitness Account
Profile
Interview
Book Review
Arts Review

Letters
Thank-You Letter
Letter for Social Change
Introductory Letter
Business Letter
Letter of Inquiry
Letter of Complaint
Cover Letter

Other
Memo
Directions
Resume
Recipe
Travel Brochure
Parody
Infographic

Other Arts: Visual/Auditory
Painting
Sculpture
Photograph
Collage
Song

A Step Further: Purpose, Audience, and Tone

Purpose: Once students understand the concept of genre, guide them to question an author's purpose. Ask questions like, "In writing this article, what was the author trying to do? Entertain? Inform? Persuade?"

Audience: Next, ask students for whom the piece is intended. Adults? Children? Then get even more specific about the audience: Is the text meant for people educated in a certain field? Athletes? Parents?

Tone: Finally, see if students can label the tone of the text. Tone is a nuanced and sophisticated concept, but students can get the gist of it with practice. Post a list of commonly employed tones somewhere in the classroom. Some ideas appear at the right.

TONES	
Enthusiastic	Sarcastic
Angry	Defeated
Apathetic	Encouraging
Bitter	Humorous
Surprised	Detached
Hopeful	Humble

I realize that it might be difficult to label an entire novel, for example, with a single tone, but engaging in the practice will help students hone this skill. Eventually, they will begin to approach everything they read and see not as empty vessels to be filled with knowledge but as active questioners ready to engage in a dialogue with the author.

50 Common Core Reading Response Activities © 2014 by Marilyn Pryle, Scholastic Teaching Resources

Allusion Wall of Fame

What It Is: Wall space covered in allusions students encounter throughout the year

Use It With: Fiction and nonfiction from all print and nonprint sources

Allusions are a part of our daily lives; they appear in news reports, television shows, movies, and common banter. For example, every time you refer to your Achilles' heel, you make an allusion to the Greek myth of the doomed Achilles, who became nearly invulnerable when his mother, Thetis, dipped his infant body into the river Styx. Alas, she held Achilles by the heel tendon, the one spot that did not receive the river's immortal powers. Allusions knit together the past and the present. Helping students understand allusions and appreciate their value will not only make them better scholars but better human beings as well.

MATERIALS
✓ Construction paper, markers, and decorative materials
✓ Tape

DIRECTIONS

* List any allusions in your reading and have students research their sources before they read the text. Allusions could include names of people, places, ideas, or events.

* Have students write or type the allusions on paper and decorate them; choose one to display on the Allusion Wall of Fame.

* *Optional*: Ask students to bring in allusions they find outside of school and explain them to the class. You can motivate students with extra credit points or public recognition by posting their names with their allusions.

Although the allusions we use seem virtually uncountable, here are just a few of the most well-known topics:

Mythology: Helen of Troy, "the face that launched a thousand ships"; Trojan Horse; golden calf; Pandora's box; Herculean feat; Nemesis; narcissist; Echo; "Midas touch"

Modern Culture: Kryptonite; "Luke, I am your father"; Scrooge

Religion: Adam and Eve; Mecca; Noah; manna from heaven; sacred cow; David and Goliath; good Samaritan; garden of Eden

Legends and Fables: Sword in the stone; Lancelot and Guinevere; the boy who cried wolf

Shakespeare: Dogs of war; sound and fury; method in the madness; green-eyed monster; Romeo; "Et tu, Brute?"

Historical: Benedict Arnold; sell down the river; shot heard 'round the world

Did You Know?
The word *panic* comes from the frenetic war cry of the goat-footed Greek god Pan.

The word *allusion* comes from the Latin word *allusio* meaning "to sport with" or "to play," as in, "to play on words."

No Room for a Wall of Fame? Try a Door of Fame or a Corner of Fame. If you can't spare any physical space, have students keep an Allusion Journal or even an Allusion List at the back of their notebooks. Any attention you can draw to allusions will help students better understand the current text and future texts, and open up our language and cultural legacy a bit more for them.

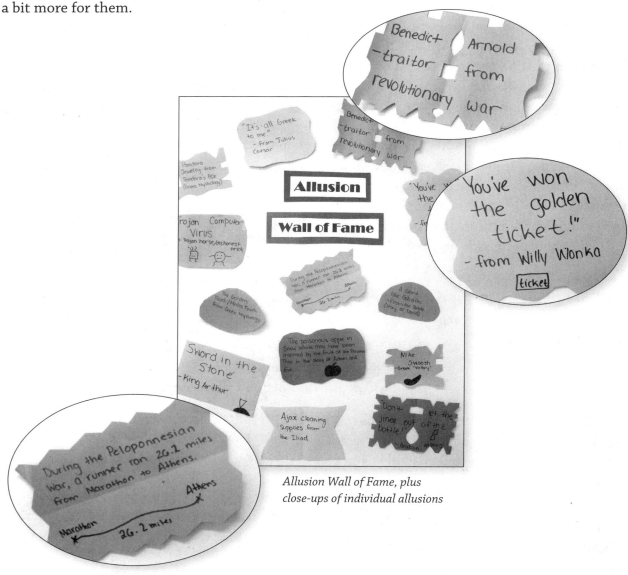

Allusion Wall of Fame, plus close-ups of individual allusions

50 Common Core Reading Response Activities © 2014 by Marilyn Pryle, Scholastic Teaching Resources

Own the Text: Annotate

What It Is: A practice of noting thoughts in the text

Use It With: Any genre of text or graphic

Good readers often make annotations to help them make sense of a text or graphic. In addition, annotation visually breaks down the text for students so that important moments and phrases stand out like physical milestones. Most important, marking up the text or graphic helps students take ownership; reading is an interactive dialogue between writer and reader, and writing their thoughts on the text or graphic helps students claim their half of the conversation.

MATERIALS

✓ Different colors of pens, pencils, and/or highlighters

✓ Overhead projector, document camera, or interactive whiteboard

A Smaller Solution

Annotating takes time. Shorter pieces like poems and articles are easily annotated, but doing an entire novel can be daunting. Try this for a longer work: Have students annotate just two pages once or twice a week. They won't be marking up every page, but they can still practice their close reading skills once a chapter or so.

DIRECTIONS

* Give a copy of a text or graphic to each student.

* Model how to annotate the text or graphic.

* Tell students to make notes; underline; draw stars, arrows, circles, or squares; and add question marks or exclamation points.

CC CONNECTION!

Marking up a text helps students "read closely" and "cite specific textual evidence" (R.1). Depending on a student's notes, she might recognize themes (R.2), plot development (R.3), word meanings (R.4), text structure (R.5), or point of view (R.6).

Learning how to be an effective annotator takes practice. At first, students usually underline almost everything. Through modeling, you can demonstrate effective annotation. I often tell students not to underline anything without writing a comment or label in the margin. Thus, instead of mindlessly underlining things with the thought, *This seems important but I don't know why*, students must analyze why they made an annotation. The label could be as basic as "simile" or "new character"; it could be as sophisticated as "theme" or "rhetorical question." At the very least, I tell students to keep a running summary on the outside margin so they can flip through the text and find important spots later. This fully engages students in that writer-reader dialogue by recognizing techniques, asking in-depth questions, and making connections to previous texts and other cultural media. The more students can actively unpack a text and assimilate it into their thinking, the more refined their thinking will be, both inside and outside school.

"What Should I Write?" At the beginning, students often ask what kinds of notes they should write. While the goal is for them to become fully autonomous in digesting a text by writing notes and symbols that are meaningful to them, it helps to give some suggestions

> **Color Code!**
>
> Give each annotation "topic" its own color—character traits could be blue, themes red, settings yellow, and so on. That way, students can easily revisit specific ideas.

reappear later in vocabulary-in-context questions, and if students already have a definition in mind, they are less likely to be fooled by the multiple-choice decoys.

initially. You may want to hang a poster with ideas, like the ones shown below.

A Step Further: Use Annotations as a Springboard for RRs

After students have marked up a text, they can then review their notes and choose one or two to develop into fully formed Reading Responses (see page 6). Annotation lends itself beautifully to the crafting of RRs because the text is right there, and students have plenty of thoughts to choose from. They can be picky in selecting the one or two ideas that move them the most.

Students Should Annotate Tests, Too: Students should get in the habit of annotating their assessments on reading passages and test questions, just as they would with a text in class. They should cross out wrong answers so they don't constantly reread those answers. Not only does annotating help students dissect the test and uncover correct answers, it also helps them take charge of the test. Instead of feeling like victims, students will feel like well-equipped readers who know how to approach a test.

Test Tip: Whenever students find an underlined word in a reading passage on a test, they should jot down a guess about its meaning while they read. These words usually

POSTER IDEAS

*IMPT (+ Why)	?? (+ Why)
Theme	Simile/Metaphor
Agree!	Irony
Allit.	Connect: _____
Disagree! (+ Why)	*CLAIM*
Char Trait	Setting
Conflict	*SYMBOL*
WHY??	Predict: _____

Sample Marginalia Poster

50 Common Core Reading Response Activities © 2014 by Marilyn Pryle, Scholastic Teaching Resources

ID the Verb (Test Prep)

What It Is: Students underline verbs on test questions

Use It With: Tests with any genre

To prepare students for the phrasing of standardized tests, craft your own tests and quizzes in the language of your state's test and of the Common Core.

MATERIALS

✓ copy of CCSS English Language Arts Standards (http://www.corestandards.org/ELA-Literacy/); practice questions from your state's assessment tests

Read through the Common Core and highlight all the verbs in the standards; do the same with some practice questions from your state assessment. (State tests can usually be found online; old tests are often published for practice use as well.) Make students aware of these verbs and have them practice what each one is asking.

> ### Post It!
> Put these test verbs on a poster so students can refer to them all year.

Let me emphasize that I know all our teaching already does this! However, students often panic or blank out on test questions and don't realize they know how to "identify" or "determine" or "relate." After practicing with verbs like these, students will feel much more

> ### CC CONNECTION!
> By identifying verbs in test questions, students must "read closely to determine what the text says explicitly" (R.1).

> ### TEST VERBS
>
> | | | |
> |---|---|---|
> | indicate | convey | describe |
> | analyze | summarize | relate |
> | define | determine | identify |
> | influence | evaluate | imply |
> | support | interpret | assess |
> | integrate | | |

comfortable and confident when taking the test. Some of the most commonly used verbs on standardized tests appear in the box above.

A Step Further: Make It Worth Their While!

On your assessments, build in points both for the correct answer as well as for identifying the verb. For example, if each correct answer is worth 5 points, adjust it so that the actual answer is worth 4 points and underlining the verb in the question is worth 1 point. Besides becoming motivated to locate the verb, students will develop the habit of underlining verbs on tests—a valuable skill during the actual state assessment.

Concrete Found Poems

What It Is: An image made up of words from text *(after reading)*

Use It With: Fiction, drama, nonfiction

I'm combining two poetic forms here: the "concrete" or shaped poem that middle school students are probably very familiar with, and the "found" poem, which they may not know. Each is a legitimate form in its own right; each can be done with sophistication and deeper meaning. Combining them can push students' thinking and analysis to a higher level.

MATERIALS

✓ Sheets of white paper and/or construction paper

✓ Pens, markers, crayons

✓ Assignment: Concrete Found Poem for each student, p. 31

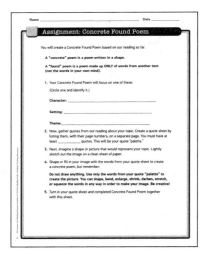

CC CONNECTION!

To create the poems described here, students must "read closely" and "cite specific textual evidence" (R.1). Depending on what type of poem they create, students might focus on a theme (R.2), character (R.3), or setting.

DIRECTIONS

To create a concrete found poem, students must only use words, phrases, or even whole sentences "found" in their text. They must shape these words into a visual representation on paper. They are not drawing; they must arrange the words, phrases, or sentences into a picture on the page. There are several ways to do this, as you'll see on the following pages.

Concrete Found Poem

Concrete Poem

A poem that visually takes the shape of its subject on the page

It may use repeating words, or it may express full thoughts and sentences.

Found Poem

A poem composed solely of words from another text

The poet can use only words "found" in that text and cannot supply others.

Character Concrete Found Poem

Students should look for words or phrases that describe a character. They can be the narrator's words, the character's own words, or another character's words, but they must appear in the text. They can be phrases about the character's physical traits ("eyes like blue ice" or "paws for hands") or traits that are either indirectly or directly stated ("You guys are heroes," "You dig sunsets okay," or "I get A's in school"). Remind students not to simply label the character with his or her traits; though these may be accurate, they must use words directly from the text.

Once students have a "palette" of words and phrases and corresponding page numbers from the text, they should create a visual representation of the character in their minds. This will determine the shape of the poem: Will it be in the shape of the character's face or full body, or will it be in the shape of a symbol for that character? Then students can create that shape strategically using the words from their palette. For example, "eyes like blue ice" could be written in an oval several times until it looks like an eye; "curly brown hair" could be written in many coils springing from a head; and "You dig sunsets okay" could be shaped into a heart. Students may find they need to consult the text for more descriptions.

Setting Concrete Found Poem

The process is the same as in the Character Concrete Found Poem, except here students look for words pertaining to a setting within the text. You might have students work in pairs, each with a different setting. When the poems are finished, the settings in the text will be represented visually and with direct quotations.

Conflict Concrete Found Poem

Students first identify a conflict in the text and then figure out a physical representation for it. Their "picture" could be of two characters fighting or yelling, one character struggling

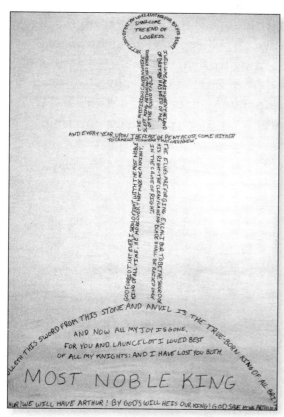

Character Concrete Found Poem

Conflict Concrete Found Poem

Jigsaw It! As an alternative to assigning one type of concrete found poem to the entire class, you could assign a separate one to small groups. As each group presents its concrete found poem, the rest of the class will learn about the other types of poems—characters, settings, conflicts and themes—from their peers.

Can these poems be done with nonfiction? Absolutely! An autobiography, for example, will have characters, settings, conflicts, and themes. At first glance, a persuasive essay may not seem appropriate; however, its claim could make for an interesting thematic concrete found poem. Students could think of a symbol and a corresponding shape for the claim, and create it with the author's persuasive phrasing, reasons, and examples. The poem would be an effective way to summarize the piece and delineate textual support.

within her own mind; a fire, storm, or some other natural disaster; and so on. The representation could be symbolic, such as a fist, door, or highway crossroads. Students should then create the picture using quotes that support the conflict.

Theme Concrete Found Poem

This category is a bit more complex, since students will have to identify a theme, create a symbol for it, and find quotes that relate to the theme. Since themes are not physical entities (like people or places), students have to think of a symbolic representation of the theme. Quotes that build the theme might be peppered throughout the story, so students may have to search large stretches of text. However, when they finish their poems, students will have not only identified a theme and supported it with in-text citations, they will also have dealt with it on a metaphorical, symbolic level, one of the most sophisticated measures of thinking.

Assignment: Concrete Found Poem

You will create a Concrete Found Poem based on our reading so far.

A "concrete" poem is a poem written in a shape.

A "found" poem is a poem made up ONLY of words from another text (not the words in your own mind).

1. Your Concrete Found Poem will focus on one of these:

   (Circle one and identify it.)

   Character: _____

   Setting: _____

   Theme: _____

2. Now, gather quotes from our reading about your topic. Create a quote sheet by listing them, with their page numbers, on a separate page. You must have at least _____ quotes. This will be your quote "palette."

3. Next, imagine a shape or picture that would represent your topic. Lightly sketch out the image on a clean sheet of paper.

4. Shape or fill in your image with the words from your quote sheet to create a concrete poem, but remember:

   Do not draw anything. Use only the words from your quote "palette" to create the picture. You can shape, bend, enlarge, shrink, darken, stretch, or squeeze the words in any way in order to make your image. Be creative!

5. Turn in your quote sheet and completed Concrete Found Poem together with this sheet.

Postcard Home

What It Is: A postcard from one character to another *(during and after reading)*

Use It With: Fiction, drama, autobiography

The simple idea of creating a postcard can get students inside a character's head. Since main characters are often on a journey of some kind, the postcard could be written to someone at home—a parent, sibling, or friend. I like to think of the recipient as someone "on the outside"— connected in some way but not directly in the narrative at the moment, or at all.

MATERIALS
✓ Sheets of white paper and/or construction paper
✓ Pens, markers, crayons

DIRECTIONS

* Assign a specific recipient ("Have Percival write a postcard to his mother") or give only general guidelines ("Have exiled Lancelot write to someone who is still in Camelot").

* When writing the postcard, students should use the first-person point of view to refer to events in the story, though they can fill in the gaps with their own imagination, as long as they stay true to the character's traits.

If you want to be more specific, or if you want to be sure each student touches upon setting, conflict, and theme, you could give brainstorming questions like these:

Postcard Brainstorming Questions

Where are you?

Do you like it? Why or why not?

What has happened to you so far? (one or two sentences)

CC CONNECTION!

By writing in the voice of a character to someone he/she has not seen lately, students must understand what the text says explicitly and implicitly (R.1) and "analyze how and why individuals [and] events . . . develop" (R.3).

What are you struggling with?

What have you learned so far about yourself or others?

What will you do?

How do you feel about the recipient?

With these questions, students must also summarize, evaluate, and predict—all in the voice of a character, which demonstrates a high level of comprehension of the story. On the front of their postcard, students should, of course, draw a picture. This will further demonstrate their understanding of setting.

Variations

Write a Postcard From the Outside In:
I do this later in the text, after students have already done a postcard from a character to someone outside the story—from the inside out. This time, students write another postcard from the "outside in"—from someone outside the story to a character still active in the narrative. The postcard could be a response from the original recipient, but it need not be; it could be from a different family member or a formerly active character who has left or died. From this perspective, students again touch upon story events, but they also have the freedom to ask questions of the main

50 Common Core Reading Response Activities © 2014 by Marilyn Pryle, Scholastic Teaching Resources

character (the recipient), give advice, and issue warnings. As before, students should illustrate this postcard.

Give Students a Postcard With the Picture Already on It:
I learned this idea in a conference session led by representatives from the Smithsonian American Art Museum. As an alternative to having kids create postcards from scratch, give them a postcard with an image on the front. Find one that represents something in the book—a setting, theme, or an event. This can take some legwork, but remember that the pictures do not have to be exact representations. For example, if the class is reading the "The Golden Apple" myth, any wedding symbol—a flowered archway, two rings, a wedding cake—would work. You could use historical photos—for example, any of the well-known Depression-era photos would be suitable with a reading of Karen

Hesse's *Out of the Dust* (1997). And of course, you could use a well-known painting whose subject fits your text exactly, such as Brueghel's *Landscape With the Fall* of Icarus when reading Ovid's "Daedalus and Icarus" from the *The Metamorphoses* (1993).

Students choose a writer and recipient related to the story and relevant to the picture. If students have done the postcard assignment once or twice, giving them the picture first is a nice twist!

BUILD A RUBRIC
A minimum number of facts from text
Appropriate voice and tone for character
A minimum length/number of sentences
Apt image
Creativity
Grammar, spelling, mechanics

Dear Dad,

Right now we are at Yellowstone National Park. This trip has been very exciting and I have seen many things. We have seen Indian dances and Lake Michigan. Spending time with Gram and Gramps has been very special. Although I am having such a great time I do miss you and Phoebe back home very much. I am very excited to finish mom's road trip journey. I am also very excited to get to mom on her birthday and bring her home so everything would go back to how it used to be and we would all stay happy forever.

Love,
Sal

Dear Mother,

The world outside our woods is breathtaking! I can't believe you didn't tell me about all of this. I miss you, but I know it is in my blood to become a knight. All that training you gave me with the darts paid off. I have earned a suit of armor. I miss your cooking.

Mother, I have seen the Holy Grail! The World is so much more complex than I imagined it being. You should come see it — it is so beautiful. I love you, but I am never coming home.

Love, your son,
Percival

Above: A postcard from Sal to her dad, from Walk Two Moons *(Creech, 1994)*

At right: A postcard from Percival to his mother, from King Arthur and His Knights of the Round Table *(Green, 2008)*

Character To-Do List

What It Is: A to-do list from the perspective of a character *(during and after reading)*

Use It With: Fiction, drama, autobiography

This quick and easy assignment can be done in class or as homework, and it's a fun variation of a Reading Response or another formal writing task. Like all of us, characters in stories have work to do, people to talk to, places to go, and goals to reach. What would the characters in a text include if they kept a to-do list?

DIRECTIONS

Tell students to choose a character from the text—or assign characters so all the characters are represented. Challenge them to get inside that character's head to create a to-do list. They can think about the following questions:

What does he or she have to do on a daily basis?

What does the character want to do or achieve?

What are the character's responsibilities?

What are the character's goals?

Where does the character have to go?

Whom does the character need to speak to?

Partner Up!

Students love working together on this activity. They enjoy discussing characters with each other and thinking of sometimes silly (but relevant!) tasks. You can have partners present their lists at the end of class.

Students should use actual information from the text, of course, but urge them to also infer information and supply text evidence to support their inferences. It helps to set a minimum number of tasks, such as ten. You

CC CONNECTION!

In order to create a to-do list for a character, students must "read closely . . . to determine what the text says explicitly and to make logical inferences from it" (R.1).

can suggest that if a character has a large goal on the list, that goal can be broken down into smaller tasks. For example, if a character's goal is to "win karate tournament," smaller steps might include, "practice 2 hours a day" and "watch opponents compete." This activity will measure students' comprehension, understanding of a character's underlying motives, ability to draw inferences from existing information, and ability to predict a character's future actions.

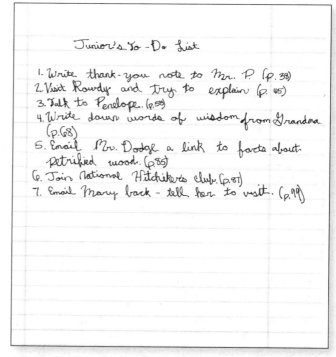

A To-Do list from Junior, the main character of Sherman Alexie's, The Absolutely True Diary of a Part-Time Indian *(2007).*

June 12 2014

Hello my name is persy Jakson. I am an
Demi god and I have a lot to do. Here are some
of the things I have to do
1 learn ancent Greek
2 Smell like a human
3 Study ancent Greee
4 go on Quest(s)
5 get back, sheld, helm of darkness and lighting bolt
6 give food to gods
7 Learn how to fight
8 Learn different stradgys
9 learn all gods and reiters
10 learn peoples weakness

To-do list for Percy Jackson in The Lightning Thief
(Riordan, 2005)

6-10-14

Journal Entry #3
Hi, my name is Percy Jackson. I am a
very young teen and have a lot of weight
on my shoulders. Here's just a few tasks I
have to accomplish......

· Find grover
· Save Thalia's tree
· make Tyson fit in
· Find magic fleece
· Stop Luke
· Help Clarisse
· Practice Swordplay
· Bring down Kronos
· Speak and ask his dad questions
· Talk sense into Luke like Hermes directed.
      Well, I have to go now and accomplish
as much as I can to make my dad proud.

To-do list for Percy Jackson in The Sea of Monsters
(Riordan, 2006)

Variations

Use Grammar: You might want to take this opportunity to require that each task begin with a present-tense verb. This not only reinforces students' knowledge of verb tense but also presents the idea of grammatical parallelism in lists, an important concept when writing.

Save the Lists: Post the to-do lists, or have students save their lists so that, as they continue reading, they can check off a task as the character completes it. If the character does not complete an item, students can jot down a note explaining why the character didn't do it.

BUILD A RUBRIC

Minimum number of tasks
Accuracy of tasks/inferences
Page citations
Grammar and spelling

Repeat It: If you do this task at the beginning of the text, repeat it again toward the end. Have students compare the two lists. They can think about how the character has changed, what new goals the character has, and what the character has learned. Use the comparisons as a springboard to a discussion about the text's themes.

Character Bucket List

What It Is: A list of goals a character wants to accomplish in his or her lifetime *(during and after reading)*

Use It With: Fiction, drama, autobiography

The Character Bucket List is, of course, a type of to-do list. However, it is not a daily, errand-running, responsibilities-are-nagging-at-you kind of to-do list; it is an end-of-life to-do list. To create a bucket list for a character, students must imagine that character's grandest goals, interests, and dreams. They must use direct information from the text and make inferences based on that information.

DIRECTIONS

As with the Character To-Do List on page 34, I recommend setting a minimum number of items for the Character Bucket List, such as ten. This will ensure that students think past the first few obvious answers.

* Let students choose a character or give them character assignments.

* To create their bucket lists, tell students to think about the following questions:

What are the character's largest goals?

What would the character do if he or she could do anything?

If the character could visit any place on Earth (or beyond), which places would he or she go to?

What hobbies or sports could you see this character trying?

What famous people would this character want to meet?

What experiences would this character have, if he or she could do anything?

What classes would the character take? What would the character want to learn about?

What accomplishments could you see the character achieving in his or her lifetime?

A Step Further: Reason Bubbles

To create an even more in-depth assignment, have students attach a "reason bubble" to each item on the bucket list. The reason bubbles would explain why the character would want to achieve the items on the list. This will ensure that students are making inferences based on actual information in the text and not just generating a random list.

Extra Challenge: Cite the Page

Have students cite a page number for each item on their list. The page number could be the literal citation of the item, or it could reference the information that led students to the inference they used to create the item. Either way, students are compelled to base their reasoning on the text itself.

BUILD A RUBRIC
Minimum number of tasks
Grammar and spelling

Host an Event

What It Is: An interactive invitation to an event, with a character as the host (*during reading*)

Use It With: Fiction, including drama; autobiography

For this activity, one should be familiar with the Evite Web site, a business that lets people email invitations for an event and manage the responses. The host and guests can leave comments; guests can add other guests or volunteer to bring items. As I was creating an Evite invitation for my own family, I thought of the mythical Eris, goddess of chaos and troublemaking, who was purposely snubbed at the wedding of Thetis and Peleus, and I mused about how that would play out on an Evite page. I then realized that it would be interesting for any literary character to send out and respond to an invitation to an event.

MATERIALS
- ✓ Hard copies of the Evite Web pages (http://www.evite.com)
- ✓ Assignment sheet (see below)
- ✓ Posterboard or large sheets of paper (legal or butcher)
- ✓ Lined notebook paper for notes and draft
- ✓ Pens, markers, crayons

DIRECTIONS

Have students create a draft in steps 1–5 before producing a final poster.

Display and/or distribute an assignment sheet like the one below to students.

1. Create an event and decide which character would host it. Based on the text so far, think of an event that would fit the story. This event should not be one that

---

> ### CC CONNECTION!
> By creating an event, guest list, replies, and comments, students will demonstrate comprehension of the text explicitly and inferentially (R.1).

appears in the text—you should invent one. It might be a birthday party, surprise party, or going-away party. It might be the celebration of an anniversary. It can be any celebration or gathering that fits the text.

Next, ask yourself which character is the most logical host for this party. Write the event and host on your draft.

2. Create a guest list. Which characters in the text should be invited to this event? Who should not be invited? Make a list, leaving about five lines of space between each character.

3. Decide if each guest would respond "Yes," "No," or "Maybe." Use the text to help you figure out who would actually attend, who would not (because of a conflict or another reason), and who would be undecided.

> ### Partner Up!
> This is a fun activity for partners. Students can work together to come up with clever comments and replies.

4. Have each guest leave a comment. Each guest, whether attending, not attending, or undecided, should leave a comment. The comments need not be long—just a sentence or two to reveal each character's true feelings. Maybe a character is so excited about the event she can hardly contain herself; maybe a character shares what he will bring or wear; maybe a character leaves a sarcastic remark when he turns down the invitation; maybe a character expresses doubt about or fear of another character. Use explicit and implicit information from the text. Do not write any comment that you cannot defend by pointing to evidence in the text. Make notes of the characters' comment on your draft.

5. Have guests reply to one another's comments. Write at least one reply from another character to each guest's initial comment. You can write more than one reply to each comment, but these replies should show how the characters feel about one another. Remember, the host can also jump in on the conversation. You can reference actual events that happen in the text. Add your replies to your draft.

6. Create your Invitation page. On your posterboard or butcher paper, write the event at the top with a short description underneath and the name of the host. Below that, list each guest and his or her response (attending or not) and comment. Then write the responses of the other characters to that comment. If you'd like to, decorate the page with the party's theme.

BUILD A RUBRIC
Event title, description, host
Minimum number of guests with attendance response
Insightful comment from each guest
Replies to each guest's comment
Demonstrated knowledge of text
Effort, creativity

You're Invited!

Join me, Pandora, for a Neighborhood Clean-Up!

I accidentally let all the evils out into the world... come help me clean them up! You'll be helping yourself and all humans of the future.

Plus, we'll have snacks and music after!

Where: Pandora and Epimetheus's house
When: ASAP

Guest	RSVP?	Comment
• Epimetheus	Yes	I wish you hadn't done this. **Pand:** I couldn't help it! Hera gave me curiosity!
• Hermes	Maybe	I told you not to open the box when I gave it to you! **Pand:** This is all your fault!
• Zeus	No	Humans will get what they deserve. **Prom:** Not fair. **Zeus:** Is eternity not long enough for you??
• Hera	Yes	Don't expect me to actually clean anything. I just want to watch. My gift of curiosity worked out the way I wanted ☺
• Hephaestus	Yes	I created you, so I will try to help. **Pand:** Thanks Dad. ♥ **Heph:** I'm not exactly your dad; I just made you from clay.
• Apollo	Yes	I'll bring the lyre.
• Athena	Maybe	Might be late; I'm going to a weaving contest.
• Aphrodite	Yes	What should I wear? **Ath:** Get over yourself! Looks aren't everything!
• Prometheus	No	Can't....talk....liver ... being...eaten...

A computer-generated invitation to an event hosted by Pandora

50 Common Core Reading Response Activities © 2014 by Marilyn Pryle, Scholastic Teaching Resources

Texting Rewrite

What It Is: A rewrite of a small- to medium-size portion of the text as a text message with appropriate slang and acronyms *(during or after reading)*

Use It With: Fiction, drama, poetry, nonfiction, autobiography, letters

By "text message," I mean the texts students tap out with their thumbs every day on their phones. Students find this activity hilarious—they love the idea that Dumbledore might write "BTW" when advising Harry, or Lancelot might write "YOLO" as he rides into battle. They are excited to create the chain of texts, and to do so, they must reread and study the dialogue closely, which is my goal!

MATERIALS
✓ Sheets of white paper
✓ Crayons or markers
✓ Document camera (optional)

DIRECTIONS

This activity works especially well when students work in pairs. After you've read a chunk of text—particularly a pivotal moment in a story or a section packed with dialogue—have students rewrite the dialogue (actual or inferred) as a text message. This means using all the abbreviations, intentional misspellings, and acronyms they normally employ when writing to friends—however, they must stay true to the meaning of the reading.

Texting acronyms fascinate me. They somehow mean more than the literal words they represent; they take on a life of their own. Often texting acronyms comment upon the message, instead of communicating the message itself. When someone texts "ROTFL," she is most likely not actually "rolling on the floor laughing" but commenting on the humor of the message.

CC CONNECTION!

In order to rewrite dialogue in "texting" language, students must "determine what the text says explicitly" and inferentially (R.1).

Additionally, acronyms can provide a visual or a sense of action: Shortis (2001) claims that "ROTFL" "is a means of animating text with stage directions" (p. 60). Thanks to the texting phenomenon, we can use this rewriting activity to see if students can read on a deeper level by making the appropriate inferences in order to apply the most apt (or clever) texting acronym. *One note:* Every time I do this activity, I find myself googling new acronyms! As with any language, texting is constantly evolving; be ready to evolve with it.

Small Groups

You could assign one chunk of the text to the entire class or form small groups and give a different chunk to each one.

A Step Further: Create Screen Shots

Have students rewrite their finished text message exchanges to look like actual screen shots, with text bubbles of different shades. The humor and impact of text messages will come across in their visual presentations. Display the screen shots so everyone can read them, or ask individual students, pairs, or small groups to exchange screen shots and to rotate until the finished products have made it around the room. And of course, the text messages can be read aloud, but I think that diminishes the "feel" of them because they are meant to be seen and not heard.

Create a Catalog

What It Is: A booklet or list of items for sale with descriptions, pictures, and pricing (*after reading*)

Use It With: Fiction, drama, autobiography

Assign this activity toward the end of a longer text, when students can recognize important objects and symbols throughout it. Students create a catalog of sale items in the text. In doing so, they demonstrate the depth of their understanding of the text.

MATERIALS

✓ A collection of print and digital catalogs

✓ Chart paper and marker or interactive whiteboard

✓ Sheets of white paper and construction paper

✓ Markers, crayons, pens

✓ Glue or tape

✓ Computer and printer (optional)

DIRECTIONS

* Let students browse through the catalogs and determine for themselves what makes a catalog successful. Create a list of the characteristics of a successful catalog.

* Explain to students that they will create their own catalogs showing items for sale from the text. It helps if you set a minimum number. Let students choose items from the entire text, or assign different sections to different pairs or groups and then compile all catalogs into a comprehensive product. Encourage students to look for actual items in the text and invent items that could fit with it, but emphasize that all items must relate to the text in a meaningful way.

CC CONNECTION!

In order to create a catalog of items from the text, students must read closely to notice details and make inferences (R.1).

Bonus: By examining catalogs, students are "analyz[ing] the structure of texts" (R.5) and "evaluat[ing] content presented in diverse media and formats" (R.7).

---

* Ask students to write a description for each item. You might want to set a minimum number of sentences for this, such as three. Students should not only reference the text in each description but also reveal the item's significance in the text. The tone of the catalog, however, is up to them: perhaps a description is sales-oriented, regretful (if the item was difficult to give up), or resigned (if the item had a good life but now must be passed on). Finally, for fun, students can set a price for each item, further indicating its worth in the text.

Tone

This is an opportunity for you to do a quick lesson on tone, showing the class different catalog descriptions for the same item in various tones.

* Tell students to reference each item with a page number from the text. "Invented" items should be cited with the page that gives the information that led students to make the inference. You could even have students use reason bubbles along the sides of the items to explain their thinking.

---

50 Common Core Reading Response Activities © 2014 by Marilyn Pryle, Scholastic Teaching Resources

✳ Have students order or group the items in a logical way. Should they be listed chronologically as they appear in the text? Grouped by similar characteristics? Grouped by the character they relate to?

✳ Tell students to create a final copy, in booklet form, either written by hand or typed on a computer. They should attach an illustration for each item and decide on a title for the catalog.

You'll be amazed by your students' creativity. Don't be surprised if they include a "rare photo" of a certain scene or person in the text, or a character's "playlist" of favorite songs—items that do not appear in the text but could very well have. To invent these items and present them in the catalog, students have to read closely and make inferences about the text.

BUILD A RUBRIC
Minimum number of items
Number of items in story
Number of items invented
Page citation for each item
Description for each item
Reason bubbles
Illustration for each item
Name for the catalog
Creativity, presentation, effort
Mechanics and spelling

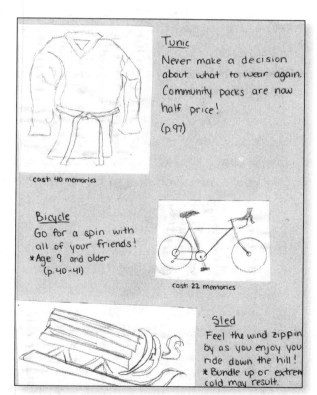

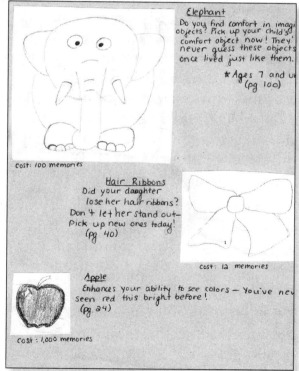

Pages from a catalog made from Lois Lowry's, The Giver *(1993).*

Haiku Chain

What It Is: A collaborative writing review activity *(during or after reading)*

Use It With: All genres of fiction and nonfiction

This activity is inspired by ancient Japanese *renga* parties, during which participants would collaborate on poetry by passing poems among groups to add more lines and keep the poems going. Apparently, these parties went on all night! In the classroom, we skip the late hours (and the sake) but keep the fun in this practice.

MATERIALS

✓ Samples of haikus

✓ Sheets of lined paper for each pair

DIRECTIONS

* Introduce or review haikus. Although modern philosophies differ on whether haikus in English must keep to the 5–7–5 syllable rule, I find that students enjoy fitting their ideas into this syllabic construct. It's what makes this activity a bit of a challenge, and therefore, fun. In addition, passing around their work is a form of publication, and this taps into each student's desire to succeed before peers.

* Put students into pairs; depending on your class size, you might have about 10–15 sets of partners. Give a sheet of lined paper to each pair, and have them write their names at the top of the sheet.

* Tell pairs that they will be writing a haiku. Don't tell them yet that they'll be passing their work to another pair. Just tell them what the haiku should be about in relation to the text, and then let them write. You could focus the haikus on whatever fits your needs

at the moment: to produce a summary of a chapter or an entire text, an explanation of a character trait, a description of the setting, or a statement of theme. Each pair should write one 5-7-5 haiku on their sheet.

* Set aside a minute or two for a couple of pairs to read their haikus out loud.

* Instruct the pairs to pass their haikus to the pair behind them. (If pairs are scattered around the room, you may have to trace a path for passing to delineate a loose circle.) The last pair should bring their haiku to the first pair. This is always a bit chaotic at first, but after the initial pass, students get the hang of it.

* Instruct pairs to read the haiku they just received. Then they should rewrite the last line of that haiku a few lines below it. That last line is now their new first line for a new haiku on that sheet.

* Pairs should then create a second and third line to complete the new haiku. You can direct them to stick with the original content (same summary, character, setting, or theme); name a new topic (if the topic was "a character and trait" for the first haiku, make it "a theme" for the second, or if they summarized pages 10–12 in the first haiku, they could summarize pages 13–15 in the second); or let them take the haiku in whatever direction they choose, keeping

50 Common Core Reading Response Activities © 2014 by Marilyn Pryle, Scholastic Teaching Resources

within the bounds of the text. Remind them to honor the 5–7–5 count.

* When the new haiku is finished, pairs should write their initials in the margin next to the poem; this ensures accountability for content as sheets circulate.

* When all partners have finished creating their new haiku, they again pass it to the pair behind them. The process will speed up once students understand the routine. After reading all the haikus on the sheet, students rewrite the last five-syllable line as the first line of their haiku, add two more lines to finish the new haiku, and initial it.

Ideally, students should repeat the process until each pair receives its original haiku. In doing so, students will read much information about and interpretations of the text from their peers while they create their own summaries and interpretations. In the final pass, students enjoy reading the path of haikus that stemmed from their original work.

hai·kaph·or·is·m

noun \hī-ka fə-,ri-zəm\

A haiku that is an aphorism, or a proverb. My classes invented this genre while constructing haiku chains about proverbs.

Variation

Focus on Skills Instead of Content:

Another way to use this activity is to focus on specific literary techniques. For example, your initial instruction to pairs could be to write a haiku that includes a simile in one of the lines. The haiku could be about any topic, but pairs should underline and label the simile. The passing procedure remains the same. With the second haiku, however, you might ask pairs to include and label an alliteration. A third round might include personification, the fourth onomatopoeia, and so on. Choose ten (or however many pairs you will have) skills that students should know, and write each skill on the board as a round is completed. With each pass, pairs use the most recent haiku's final line as their new first line, and continue writing—but they incorporate the new literary technique into the next two lines of the new haiku they create.

Students really enjoy this activity and like to be funny or clever in front of their classmates while still completing the work. By the last few passes, silliness has kicked in and students are eager to write the next haiku. It's one of those activities during which students forget they are learning.

Twitter Posts

What It Is: A 140-character post about a text *(during or after reading)*

Use It With: Fiction and nonfiction, all genres

I love Twitter and think this social media site holds a great deal of educational potential. The many articles written about ways to use Twitter in the classroom are accessible via a simple online search. For this activity, however, neither you nor your students even need a Twitter account; all you need to know is the main premise behind every post.

MATERIALS

✓ Strips of paper

✓ Posterboard and markers (optional)

✓ Gold star stickers (optional)

DIRECTIONS

Twitter's foremost rule is that every "tweet" must be no longer than 140 characters, including spaces. This assignment has students compose a short tweet-length response to their current reading. You could even create a "Twitter Feed" poster to display the tweets. Here are some ideas for students to tweet about:

Extra Challenge: Use a Quote

Amp up the tweet by requiring students to include a quote! (Obviously, the quote would have to be concise, only a few words or a phrase. I recommend that students squeeze a page number in as well.) The tweet could include:

A quote that illustrates a character trait

A quote illustrating a theme

A quote including any literary technique, such as simile, imagery, alliteration, or allusion

A quote of some key words about setting or mood

You can be very specific with the topic. For example, assign tweets for "quotes about Jonah," "quotes that show courage," or "quotes

FICTION TWEET IDEAS	NONFICTION TWEET IDEAS
• Summary of chapter/night's reading/entire text	• Opinion of text
• Theme of text	• Agree/disagree with author
• A character and three traits	• Specify essay genre and how you identified it
• A description of setting	• Alternative title
• Any symbol and its meaning	• Tweet to author
• A prediction	• Rewrite final sentence
	• Write opposite view of claim

Make It Almost Real!

Have students identify themselves on tweets with the @ symbol and their names, omitting spaces.

that begin a flashback." Several students may find the same quotes, but there should be some variety and depth in the responses.

Tip: Be Concise! One trick I share with students is to write out what they want to say, and then start trimming until they pare it down to 140 characters. This practice forces students to examine repetition in their own thoughts and writing, and to cut extraneous words and phrases.

#UseHashtags: I think the hashtag is a wonderful teaching and learning tool. Hashtags are part of the tweet and count as characters, but they are also separate from it in a way. Using a hashtag requires the writer to step outside the tweet and view the thought in a larger conversation. This larger conversation is not just about the text or even literature itself—it could be about any discipline or topic in the world! A hashtag can represent a category relative to the tweet, such as in this example: *It's so unfair that Cassie was whipped for not taking the used book! #injustice*

A hashtag can also be a comment on the tweet itself. Students often use the hashtag humorously—it's an opportunity for them to add a funny note about their own thoughts or the text itself. The hashtag can be a word or an entire phrase without spaces, such as this example: *Snape almost killed Harry during the Quiddich match! #whatabully.*

Teacher Tweets: Post your own tweets on the board or Twitter Feed poster to set the topic for the day or to model the category of tweets you're assigning. Add a funny hashtag. Kids love this and will be motivated to participate.

Favorites and Retweets: Twitter users can "favorite" a tweet they like. When this happens, a gold star appears in the corner of the tweet.

Keep a stash of gold stars that students can put on tweets they like on the Twitter Feed poster. Additionally, you can have students "retweet" the best tweets by copying them down in a notebook (have them reserve a back page for retweets). This can help students think more deeply about important ideas in the text that they may not have noticed themselves.

A Step Further: Writing

To use this activity as a springboard for a longer work, have students link their idea to a longer writing activity. As often happens on Twitter, the tweet is merely a short summary or announcement of a longer Web page, picture, video, or article. Ask students to choose one of their tweets and to draft a paper about the characterization or theme, write or film an interview, create a collage or some other illustration, or take a poll—all related to the text. After reading a novel, for example, students can turn to their list of tweets for writing and project topics.

Another Step Further: Have Story Characters Tweet!

For a longer project, students can replicate a complete Twitter conversation in which multiple characters post, reply, and favorite each other's tweets.

How to Grade

For Twitter conversations, set a minimum number of tweets, quotes, or references to the text. You could give bonus points for giving the characters creative usernames!

For a single tweet, give a small grade or homework check for fulfilling the original requirements (such as giving a quote, having a character trait, or using a hashtag).

Text Frame Visual

What It Is: A visual representation of the story-within-a-story format (*after reading*)

Use It With: Fiction, drama, or autobiography that employs the frame format

"Frame story" describes the story-within-a-story format. Many authors structure stories in this way in order to deepen themes and build complexity within a tale. Usually, there's a place in the narrative where the stories converge, whether it be at the beginning, middle, or end. Having students create a visual of this structure helps them better understand not only the different plots but also the symbols and themes that link them.

MATERIALS

✓ Sheets of white and construction paper, boxes, and other material

✓ Markers, crayons, colored pencils

✓ Glue and tape

DIRECTIONS: COMIC-STRIP FRAMEWORK

The most basic way to do this is with comic-strip representations of each plot, with each

CC CONNECTION!

By visually depicting a story's multiple plots, students will "analyze the structure of texts, including how . . . larger portions . . . relate to each other and the whole" (R.5).

frame depicting a major event or moment. Students choose only the most important events in each story, and then attach the different comic strips (i.e., plotlines) together where they converge. The comic strips must present an accurate and succinct summary, evidence of themes, and appropriate plot connections. The photo below shows the result —an illustrated visual representation of the various plots in *The Thousand and One Nights* (1973), which looks somewhat like a crossword puzzle.

The close-up below of this comic-strip framework shows a portion of the plot, in which a fisherman relates the story of a king and a doctor to an evil genie. To complete the comic-strip visual, students had to attach each new story at the appropriate place in the previous story. In addition, they had to leave room at the end of each story to "back up" into the original story.

Comic-Strip Framework for
The Thousand and One Nights

Close-Up of Comic-Strip Framework for
The Thousand and One Nights

Extra Challenge: A Unique Framework

Students enjoyed this activity, but I decided to open it up even more. I told students there would be extra credit for any group who could figure out how to show the story-within-a-story framework in another way (and extra-extra credit for a unique framework). Any type of visual representation was okay, but they had to maintain the original requirements: an accurate and succinct summary, evidence of themes, and appropriate plot connections. From there, they could let their creative juices flow.

I was amazed by what groups turned in: storybooks inside storybooks; boxes inside boxes (with each side of the box representing a point in the summary, and arrows directing the viewer); a genie lamp whose smoke was a curving comic strip of one of the plotlines; a large layered circle symbolizing karma (a theme of the story) in which all three plots swirled and connected; and a lamp whose tip attached to a medicine jar, whose lid opened to reveal a falcon, whose wingtip looped back to the original lamp. Some groups turned in

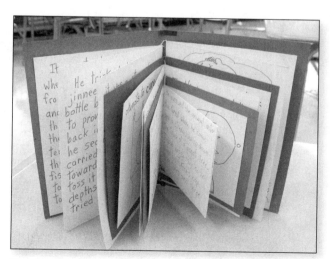

This Unique Framework features a storybook within a storybook.

actual lamps or urns with the comic strips rolled up and attached to the inside of the lids, so that when the lids were opened, the comic strips uncoiled to reveal the stories. As usual, students came up with ideas I never would have dreamed of!

DIRECTIONS: A Unique Framework

* This activity lends itself to collaboration in pairs or small groups because students will debate which events are important enough to represent on the framework. Some students will want to draw while others plan, write captions, or find quotes. Since the goal is close reading and collective writing, small groups of no more than three work best.

* Explain to groups that they will be creating a summary of the stories in the text. Display

Motivate!

I use this "bonus" technique often: students can get extra points for thinking in a new way. But I award even more points if they push themselves in this area, thinking of a way that's not only new but one-of-a-kind. Kids enjoy the challenge.

an example of the basic comic-strip format. Set a minimum number of summary points, such as five, for each story. The summaries should also include evidence of each story's theme (or another element). I suggest making an assignment sheet for students to read and refer to as they work.

* Tell groups to compose the summary points on paper before creating their visual representation. Have students quote the original story in addition to paraphrasing; for example, they could include one or more quote per plotline or per frame. And of course they should cite page numbers!

* Then have groups design their visual representations. Remind them that the stories must connect at the appropriate plot points. At this point, tell students that they can invent their own shapes and formats for the visual representation. They might use objects in the story, symbolic shapes that represent character traits or themes, or even 3-D structures.

* Finally, allow time for groups to create their designs. As with any handmade work, this activity could take several days of class time. If you can't spare that many days, set aside time during one or two classes for planning and starting time and have groups finish their representations for homework.

In the end, having a visual map of the story really helps students understand the layered-plot structure: how it works, where the stories connect, and what the unifying ideas in the text are.

Theme Road Trip

What It Is: A drawn map depicting a story theme *(after reading)*

Use It With: Fiction, autobiography, drama, ballads

Start your engines! Students will literally map a theme's progress throughout a story by buckling a theme into a car, drawing the road of the plot, and putting appropriate signposts along the way.

MATERIALS

✓ Sheets of lined notebook paper, white paper, and construction paper

✓ Crayons, markers, colored pencils

✓ Scissors

✓ Glue or tape

✓ Copies of common road signs and cars for students to cut out (optional)

Make It 3-D!
Instead of drawing the road on paper, students could make a 3-D version with standing signs, hills, trees, and a real toy car.

DIRECTIONS

* After reading a text, do a lesson identifying its themes. Ask small groups to create a list of themes with text examples to back up each of them, and present their work. (If you're pressed for time, give students a list of the themes.)

* Have partners or small groups select a theme from the list, or assign themes to ensure that each theme is represented.

* Tell students to ask themselves how their theme develops throughout the story. Give them a brainstorming sheet like the one at the right to guide them.

CC CONNECTION!
This post-reading activity helps students "determine . . . themes in a text and analyze their development" (R.2).

QUESTIONS TO GO DEEPER WITH THEME

Answer the following questions with your partner or group.

Give a page number with each answer.

1. How does the theme begin? Looking back, what could be the first event that introduces the theme?

2. What are some other early events that show that the author is trying to make this a theme?

3. Does the theme always go smoothly? What are some events that made me think the theme was struggling to stay alive?

4. Are there any events where the theme seems to have completely disappeared?

5. Does the theme ever grow deeper? Do extra examples of the theme surface as the story goes on? Do new people experience the theme?

6. Is there a moment where the theme feels strongest? What is it?

7. What do the main characters learn about the theme by the end of the text?

8. Does the theme somehow continue after the story ends, or does it end with the story? Explain.

* When students have sufficiently explored the theme, tell them that they will eventually create a map of it. But first, display the road signs and ask students to identify them. Examples could include:

  • *Stop signs • Yield signs*

  • *Red/yellow/green lights • Merge signs*

  • *Slow signs • Curvy Road Ahead signs*

  • *Caution signs (Falling Rock, Ice, Children Playing, and so on)*

  • *Speed Limit sign*

  • *Speed Bump sign*

  • *Rest Area sign*

  • *Wrong Way sign*

* Explain to students that theme is like a car driving along the road of the story. They will show how the theme travels along the road of their text. You might model how you would create your own example. Here's a sample for the theme of friendship:

  If two characters become friends easily in the beginning of a book, the road could begin with a green light. Next to it, I would write a sentence from the text with its page number. Maybe the budding friendship experiences some twists and turns; I would have the road reflect this by adding a Caution: Curves Ahead sign and a quotation. Maybe one friend hurts another: a speed bump would be appropriate. Or a new friend joins the group: I'd use a Merge sign. Perhaps the friendship abruptly ends; a red light, Stop sign, or Rest Area sign might be the best choice.

  Remind students to use their brainstorming sheet for ideas, and to add, delete, or rearrange their ideas in any logical way. Set a minimum number of examples of the theme for the map to show.

* Have students do a sketch of their map first, with possible signs and terrain. Encourage them to let the geography of the road reflect the theme's journey. For example, if the main character's friendship seems lost, students can not only put up a Caution: Dark Area sign but also draw a thick forest along either side of the road. Welcome any creative or symbolic interpretation of the theme because this will reflect a deep understanding of and higher-level thinking about the text. Remind students to show a destination, or ending point, on their map. They should ask themselves the last question in the box on page 49, "What happens to the theme at the end of the text?" and represent the answer with a signpost, terrain change, or symbol. This, of course, will involve the resolution of the plot as well. Emphasize that next to each sign or terrain change they should put a paraphrase or direct quotation and a page number.

* After students have done the rough sketch, allow time for them to create their actual map.

This activity is a fun way to help students identify a theme, locate its manifestations in a story, and analyze its progress throughout the plot. All these tasks involve abstract thinking: Creating a hands-on representation will aid students in reaching that higher-level cognition.

BUILD A RUBRIC
Theme identified clearly
Minimum number of examples of theme
Clear destination/resolution
Direct quotes/paraphrases with page numbers
Map with appropriate signposts and terrain
Effort, creativity
Grammar, spelling, mechanics

 50 Common Core Reading Response Activities © 2014 by Marilyn Pryle, Scholastic Teaching Resources

Create a Wordle

What It Is: A word collage made from a text *(before, during, and after reading)*

Use It With: All genres of fiction and nonfiction

You may be familiar with the Wordle.net Web site, and even may have made fun "word clouds" about texts. This activity explores how to use Wordle to really go deep into plot, theme, symbols, and character traits—and its special uses with drama and nonfiction.

MATERIALS

✓ Samples of Wordle collages
✓ Computers and printers
✓ Interactive whiteboard (optional)

The Premise of Wordle: The way Wordle.net processes text into a collage is an invaluable teaching tool. The Web site does not randomly arrange words into a nice-looking collage; rather, it takes the entered text and creates a "word cloud" out of the most frequently used words in that text. Additionally, it sizes the words within the Wordle: The more a word is used, the larger it is in the Wordle cloud. The size of any word, then, represents its frequency in the text. (Articles, conjunctions, and some prepositions are automatically removed). The applications of this are almost infinite! If you haven't created a Wordle before, here's how to do it:

* Go to http://www.wordle.net. Click on the Create tab.

* A large box will appear with the instructions, "Paste in a bunch of text." Although it's possible to type text into Wordle, it is far easier to cut and paste some or all of your text into the box. This means you must find your text online, or, if it is not online, type or scan your text into a document and cut and paste it from there. You could use a single chapter or page, an act, an article, or a poem.

* Click on the Go button. The Wordle will appear on the next screen. You can change the font and colors; however, you cannot print or save from the site. Once you create a Wordle, you can submit it to the site's public gallery only. I usually display the Wordle on the Smartboard in my room, or take a screenshot of it to display.

Use Wordle before or during reading or as a culminating activity. It simply depends on your purpose. Some suggestions appear on the next page.

CC CONNECTION!

Depending on how you use Wordle, you can hit upon several standards: determining "what the text says explicitly" and making "logical inferences from it" (R.1), determining "central ideas or themes" (R.2), analyzing how a story's components interact (R.3), interpreting the language of a text (R.4), and discussing point of view (R.6). And of course, you will be integrating and evaluating content in a different, visual format (R.7).

The 1-2 Punch!

Wordle activities work well when students try questions and statements like the ones shown on pages 52 and 53 alone first and then pair up to share their thoughts. This allows them to ingest the Wordle individually for a bit, letting the words and format spark ideas.

A Sample Pre-Reading Wordle

I used the Wordle below as a pre-reading activity for the final chapter in *The Outsiders*, (Hinton, 2012) in which Ponyboy reads the letter Johnny left in *Gone With the Wind* before he died. For this Wordle, I used the letter for the text. The letter is relatively brief, and so are most of the words in the Wordle. The questions I used with this Wordle appear below.

1. Which word is the largest? What do you think about that?

2. Pick out five words and guess what Johnny will say with them.

3. Find a word that relates to a past event in the story, and explain your choice.

4. Find a word that relates to a theme in the story, and explain your choice.

5. Whom does Johnny talk about the most? What does this show?

6. Write a haiku using at least four words in the Wordle.

For a challenge, have students attach page numbers to their answers.

A Sample Post-Reading Wordle

I used the Wordle on the next page as a post-reading activity with Chapter 9 of *The Outsiders*.

After displaying it, I asked students the following questions:

1. What is the biggest word in the Wordle? What does its size mean?

2. Why aren't the words "Pony" or "Ponyboy" in the Wordle?

3. How does Ponyboy being the narrator explain why certain words are the biggest?

4. What other names does Ponyboy talk about the most?

5. Find a word about one of the settings (time or place) in Chapter 9. What happened there?

6. Find a word about an action or event in Chapter 9. What happened?

7. Find a word about a theme (message) in the book. Why do you think this tells about the theme?

8. Find a word that could be a character trait for one of the characters. Explain.

9. Find a noun, an adjective, and a verb. How does each fit in the story?

Pre-Reading Wordle for The Outsiders *(Hinton, 2012)*

50 Common Core Reading Response Activities © 2014 by Marilyn Pryle, Scholastic Teaching Resources

Sample Post-Reading Wordle for The Outsiders *(Hinton, 2012)*

10. Find a word you don't understand, or you are surprised to see. What surprises you?

11. Write a sentence about the story using at least five words from the Wordle.

12. Choose a word that you haven't used yet in your answers, and use it to make a prediction about the story.

You can see from these questions the possibilities for discussion that can stem from the Wordle. Students enjoy studying the Wordle format and figuring out how the words fit. Let me again emphasize that the Wordle uses only actual words from the text, so students are, in fact, discussing the actual text at all times.

Variations

Wordles With Drama: Wordle is particularly useful with plays because characters' names will appear *twice*—in uppercase to indicate they are speaking, and with only the first letter capitalized when a character is spoken to or about. Thus, in addition to questions about plot, setting, and theme, you can ask questions about who *speaks* the most lines, and who *is spoken about* the most. Students could also search for words that are part of the stage directions. A Wordle based on Shakespeare's *The Tragedy of Julius Caesar* (n.d.) appears on the next page.

Wordles With Nonfiction: With nonfiction, you can use Wordles as a pre- or post-reading activity to identify a central idea or an argument, isolate and discuss transition words, formulate facts and opinions, and generate questions. Of course, depending on the exact genre of the nonfiction text, you might also identify people, settings, and symbols.

Have Students Create Wordles: Challenge students to create their own Wordles by choosing and inputting significant passages, character descriptions, thematic passages, descriptions of setting, or climactic passages from a text. You could also ask small groups to create a Wordle and make up their own questions to ask another group.

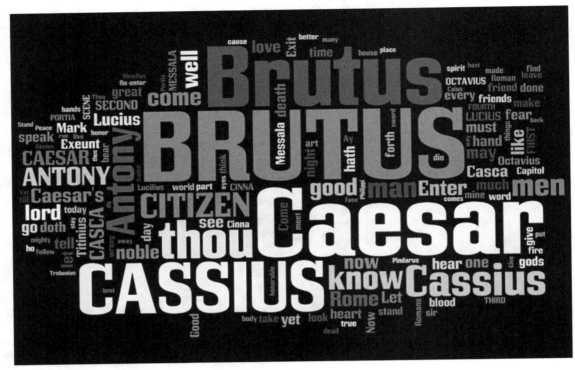

Sample Wordle for The Tragedy of Julius Caesar *(n.d.)*

OTHER IDEAS FOR USING WORDLE

- Use a passage with a distinct mood, and have students isolate the words that create that mood.

- Upload an entire book or first chapter as a way of introducing characters, setting, and conflict before doing any other pre-reading or background activity. This is a fun guessing game!

- Have students write a paragraph about themselves using words from the Wordle.

- Ask students to search for rhymes, near-rhymes, alliteration, assonance, or onomatopoeia in the Wordle.

- Have students create similes and metaphors using only Wordle words.

- Use the Wordle to reinforce not only basic parts of speech but also nuances in grammar (helping verbs, words that can be two parts of speech, verb tenses, and so on).

- Have students draw a picture about the text using captions/speech bubbles made from the Wordle.

- Have students isolate any words related to a certain dialect (Elizabethan English, Southern American English, Western American English, and so on).

- Choose a dominant symbol from the story and have students find all the words related to that symbol.

- Have students create a found poem, limerick, couplet, acrostic, or tanka with words from the Wordle.

50 Common Core Reading Response Activities © 2014 by Marilyn Pryle, Scholastic Teaching Resources

Text Element Stations

What It Is: Student-created stations about elements in a text *(during or after reading)*

Use It With: Fiction and nonfiction

This activity is student-centered, collaborative, and text-based—a best-practice trifecta! It has many variations, so you can tailor it to the needs of your class. Small groups create posters about different aspects of the text. Posters are hung around the room in stations, so students can circulate and gather information on all the text elements in the reading.

MATERIALS

✓ Text Element Poster Brainstorming Sheet for each group, p. 57

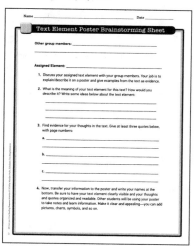

✓ Sheets of poster-size paper or butcher paper
✓ Markers

DIRECTIONS

This activity works best with pairs or small groups of up to four students, so you might want to count how many groups you will have before you make a list of text elements.

* Assign a text element to each group. Have groups use the Text Element Poster Brainstorming Sheet to discuss and brainstorm ideas about that text element in the text.

CC CONNECTION!

Depending on what you assign for each poster, students will closely read for explicit and implicit information, and cite (R.1), determine themes (R.2), and analyze interactions over the course of the text (R.3).

POSSIBLE FICTION ELEMENTS

- Characters (or Individual Characters for a large class)
- Setting (or Individual Settings)
- Foreshadowing
- Flashback
- Mood
- Conflict
- Allusions
- Plot (or Individual Plot Points, Rising Action, Climax)
- Theme(s)
- Symbols
- Figurative Language
- Point of View
- Imagery

POSSIBLE NONFICTION ELEMENTS

- Main Idea
- Structure of paragraphs
- Reasons
- Examples
- Introduction Technique
- Call to Action
- Transitions/ Transition Words
- Imagery
- Figurative Language
- Allusions
- Point of View
- Tone

* Have groups create a poster about the text element. Remind them that although the poster should be visually appealing (not cramped or sloppy), this is not an art project. The goal is to find and share information. It will probably take one class for students to find information and transfer it to the poster.

* Hang posters up around the room with plenty of space in between.

* Ask students to roam around and take notes about the information on the posters; however, in order to ensure that they "analyze how and why individuals, events, and ideas develop and interact" (R.3), I suggest that you make another handout with specific questions linking each text element. Students will have to read the posters and think, instead of copying posters word for word. Your questions will depend on what each group posted, but below are some sample questions for fiction and nonfiction.

* Discuss students' responses to the questions. Leave the posters up for reference. The beauty of this activity is that it is not a huge, official project. It is not a complete book report or scrapbook or research task. It is simply a close look at one small aspect of the text. So, instead of lecturing on the information yourself, or having students work at their desks on a series of handouts, you will have students collaborating, moving around, presenting their own small piece of the puzzle, and learning the rest from their peers.

BUILD A RUBRIC

Group Grade:

Completion of brainstorming sheet

Information on poster

Minimum number of quotations, with citations

Clarity/Appeal of poster

Individual Grade:

Completion of post-activity questions

FICTION

1. Explain how one character's trait leads to an event in the plot.
2. How does one of the flashbacks contribute to a character's trait?
3. Explain how a specific setting or certain images help set the mood for an event in the plot.
4. How does a symbol in the story relate to a theme?
5. Reread the climax. How is the conflict present in the climax?
6. How does the narrator affect the plot? Would the plot be different with a different point of view?
7. How do the allusions that the author chose relate to the characters? To the themes?
8. Look up the examples of figurative language in the text. How do they enhance the imagery?
9. Does the setting ever foreshadow an event? When? How?
10. Choose two or three posters and explain how their elements are linked.

NONFICTION

1. How do the reasons support the main idea?
2. Do the transition words enhance the structure of the paragraphs? How?
3. How does the introduction ultimately tie in to the main idea?
4. What specific images contribute to the main idea?
5. How does the point of view influence the main idea?
6. How does the point of view contribute to the tone?
7. Explain how the tone affects the call to action.
8. How does imagery influence the tone of the piece?
9. Do the introduction and conclusion link together in any way? How?
10. Choose two posters and explain how their elements are linked.

Text Element Poster Brainstorming Sheet

Other group members: _____

_____

Assigned Element: _____

1. Discuss your assigned text element with your group members. Your job is to explain/describe it on a poster and give examples from the text as evidence.

2. What is the meaning of your text element for this text? How would you describe it? Write some ideas below about the text element:

   _____

   _____

   _____

3. Find evidence for your thoughts in the text. Give at least three quotes below, with page numbers:

   a. _____

   _____

   b. _____

   _____

   c. _____

   _____

4. Now, transfer your information to the poster and write your names at the bottom. Be sure to have your text element clearly visible and your thoughts and quotes organized and readable. Other students will be using your poster to take notes and learn information. Make it clear and appealing—you can add pictures, charts, symbols, and so on.

Thank-You Letter

What It Is: A letter from one character to another, or from an author to someone who has been influential *(during or after reading)*

Use It With: Fiction and nonfiction

The thank-you letter is, alas, becoming a lost art in our culture. Of course, we still thank one another and express gratitude; we simply do it in emails and texts, and use abbreviations like "Thx!" Here, students write a thank-you note from a character or an author. You can make this activity as specific or as open as you want.

MATERIALS

✓ Assignment: Thank-You Letter (Fiction/Narrative) for each student, p. 60

✓ Assignment: Thank-You Letter (Nonfiction) for each student, p. 61

✓ Sheets of lined notebook paper

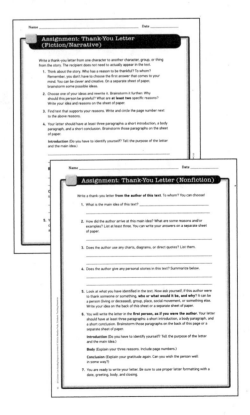

CC CONNECTION!

Writing a thank-you letter in a character's voice compels students to read closely for information and inferences (R.1) and "analyze how and why individuals . . . interact over the course of a text" (R.3).

DIRECTIONS: Fiction

You can assign the characters who will write and receive the thank-you letter. However, it's more of a challenge if you have students choose their own sender and recipient from the text. To do this, students have to ask themselves, "Who should be thanking someone?" and "Whom should that person thank, and why?"

To open up the activity even more, tell students that neither the sender nor recipient need be an actual character! Either role could be taken by a character outside the pages of the text—a relative or friend who is not part of the plot. The recipient could even be a place or an object. As long as students demonstrate a deeper understanding of the story, they can be creative and even funny with their choices of sender and recipient.

Set parameters for length, number of quotes, page numbers, and letter formatting.

In doing this activity, students must integrate their understanding of characters, events, and ideas. They may also infer how events and people outside the text influence the story. Exploring all of these relationships demonstrates a deeper understanding of the narrative.

50 Common Core Reading Response Activities © 2014 by Marilyn Pryle, Scholastic Teaching Resources

A Step Further: Try It With Nonfiction

This activity works with nonfiction as well, although this can be a little trickier. Follow the same general procedure described for fiction. With a persuasive piece, for example, students could write a letter from the author to a person or group (or even to an event) of obvious influence. In order to figure out who the recipient could be, students will have to ask themselves, "Why does the author think this way? What has influenced him or her?" and "Does the author reference specific events or quote certain people?" They will have to examine the author's examples for evidence. In doing this, students will see the larger interplay of writer, ideas, and events.

<table>
<tr><td colspan="1">BUILD A RUBRIC</td></tr>
<tr><td>Process (brainstorming sheet and drafts)</td></tr>
<tr><td>Introduction, body, and conclusion paragraphs</td></tr>
<tr><td>Two specific reasons for letter</td></tr>
<tr><td>Page numbers</td></tr>
<tr><td>Letter format</td></tr>
<tr><td>Spelling, grammar, mechanics</td></tr>
</table>

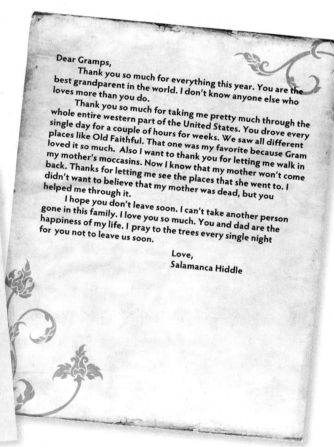

Dear Gramps,
Thank you so much for everything this year. You are the best grandparent in the world. I don't know anyone else who loves more than you do.
Thank you so much for taking me pretty much through the whole entire western part of the United States. You drove every single day for a couple of hours for weeks. We saw all different places like Old Faithful. That one was my favorite because Gram loved it so much. Also I want to thank you for letting me walk in my mother's moccasins. Now I know that my mother won't come back. Thanks for letting me see the places that she went to. I didn't want to believe that my mother was dead, but you helped me through it.
I hope you don't leave soon. I can't take another person gone in this family. I love you so much. You and dad are the happiness of my life. I pray to the trees every single night for you not to leave us soon.

Love,
Salamanca Hiddle

A thank-you letter from Sal to her grandfather in Walk Two Moons *(Creech, 1994)*

53 Farmer's Road
Euclid, Ohio

Dear Sal,
Thank you so much for everything you have done for me over the past few weeks. It was all really helpful and comforting to have you during these events.
I'm so glad to have had you by my side while my mom was missing. You did so much for me like staying over for dinner, having me stay at your house, and helping me look for clues. I found it especially helpful when you came to the police station with me.
Also thank you for being there with me when mom was coming home with the "special guest." It was really nice having you there in case things went wrong. Well, thanks for everything Sal. Hope to see you soon!

Phoebe

A thank-you letter from Phoebe to Sal in Walk Two Moons *(Creech, 1994)*

Name _____ Date _____

Assignment: Thank-You Letter (Fiction/Narrative)

Write a thank-you letter from one character to another character, group, or thing from the story. The recipient does not need to actually appear in the text.

1. Think about the story. Who has a reason to be thankful? To whom? Remember, you don't have to choose the first answer that comes to your mind. You can be clever and creative. On a separate sheet of paper, brainstorm some possible ideas.

2. Choose one of your ideas and rewrite it. Brainstorm it further: Why should this person be grateful? What are **at least two** specific reasons? Write your idea and reasons on the sheet of paper.

3. Find text that supports your reasons. Write and circle the page number next to the above reasons.

4. Your letter should have at least three paragraphs: a short introduction, a body paragraph, and a short conclusion. Brainstorm those paragraphs on the sheet of paper.

   Introduction (Do you have to identify yourself? Tell the purpose of the letter and the main idea.)

   _____

   _____

   Body (Explain your two reasons. Include your page number.)

   _____

   _____

   Conclusion (Explain your gratitude again. Can you wish the person well in some way?)

   _____

   _____

5. You are ready to write your letter. Write it in the first person, as if you are the character. Be sure to use proper letter formatting with a date, greeting, body, and closing.

Assignment: Thank-You Letter (Nonfiction)

Write a thank-you letter **from the author of this text**. To whom? You can choose!

1. What is the main idea of this text? _____

   _____

2. How did the author arrive at this main idea? What are some reasons and/or examples? List at least three. You can write your answers on a separate sheet of paper.

   _____

3. Does the author use any charts, diagrams, or direct quotes? List them.

   _____

   _____

4. Does the author give any personal stories in this text? Summarize below.

   _____

   _____

5. Look at what you have identified in the text. Now ask yourself, if this author were to thank someone or something, **who or what would it be, and why**? It can be a person (living or deceased), group, place, social movement, or something else. Write your idea on the back of this sheet or a separate sheet of paper.

6. You will write the letter in the **first person, as if you were the author**. Your letter should have at least three paragraphs: a short introduction, a body paragraph, and a short conclusion. Brainstorm those paragraphs on the back of this page or a separate sheet of paper.

   Introduction (Do you have to identify yourself? Tell the purpose of the letter and the main idea.)

   Body (Explain your three reasons. Include page numbers.)

   Conclusion (Explain your gratitude again. Can you wish the person well in some way?)

7. You are ready to write your letter. Be sure to use proper letter formatting with a date, greeting, body, and closing.

50 Common Core Reading Response Activities © 2014 by Marilyn Pryle, Scholastic Teaching Resources

Break-Up Letter

What It Is: A letter from one character to another that ends their relationship *(during or after reading)*

Use It With: Fiction

This letter is quite different from the thank-you letter in the previous chapter, but the required level of textual comprehension is the same. Instead of imagining one character thanking another, students must ask themselves which characters are ready to part ways. This separation need not be a romantic breakup. It could be a separation from a friend or a group, a movement, a place, or even an idea. Writing a break-up letter works particularly well toward the end of a novel, when the main character usually grows or changes, and leaves behind some old beliefs or people.

MATERIALS

✓ Assignment: Break-Up Letter (Fiction/Narrative) for each student, p. 63

✓ Sheets of lined notebook paper

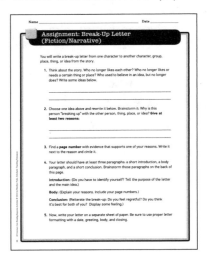

CC CONNECTION!

Like the thank-you letter, writing a break-up letter in a character's voice compels students to read closely for information and inferences (R.1) and "analyze how and why individuals . . . interact over the course of a text" (R.3).

DIRECTIONS

After passing out the assignment sheet, discuss the steps with students.

BUILD A RUBRIC
Create a rubric similar to the one for the thank-you letter on page 59. It might include:
Process (brainstorming sheet and drafts)
Introduction, body, and conclusion paragraphs
Two specific reasons for the letter
Page numbers
Letter format
Spelling, grammar, mechanics

50 Common Core Reading Response Activities © 2014 by Marilyn Pryle, Scholastic Teaching Resources

Assignment: Break-Up Letter (Fiction/Narrative)

You will write a break-up letter from one character to another character, group, place, thing, or idea from the story.

1. Think about the story. Who no longer likes each other? Who no longer likes or needs a certain thing or place? Who used to believe in an idea, but no longer does? Write some ideas below.

    _____

    _____

2. Choose one idea above and rewrite it below. Brainstorm it: Why is this person "breaking up" with the other person, thing, place, or idea? **Give at least two reasons**:

    _____

    _____

3. Find a **page number** with evidence that supports one of your reasons. Write it next to the reason and circle it.

4. Your letter should have at least three paragraphs: a short introduction, a body paragraph, and a short conclusion. Brainstorm those paragraphs on the back of this page.

    Introduction: (Do you have to identify yourself? Tell the purpose of the letter and the main idea.)

    Body: (Explain your reasons. Include your page numbers.)

    Conclusion: (Reiterate the break-up: Do you feel regretful? Do you think it's best for both of you? Display some feeling.)

5. Now, write your letter on a separate sheet of paper. Be sure to use proper letter formatting with a date, greeting, body, and closing.

50 Common Core Reading Response Activities © 2014 by Marilyn Pryle, Scholastic Teaching Resources

Domino Effect

What It Is: Plot points secured to dominoes and knocked down *(after reading)*

Use It With: Fiction, drama, ballads, autobiography, narrative nonfiction

Set up and knock down dominoes, and then ask students what this action might mean in terms of an event: What might happen if they leave their homework at home? Challenge students to go beyond the obvious—they would get a 0 but then what might happen?

MATERIALS

✓ Assignment: Domino Effect for each student, p. 65

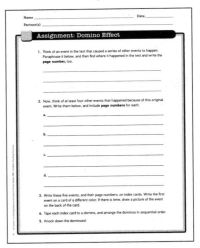

✓ Index cards of different colors
✓ Dominoes (at least 40 depending on size of class and groups)
✓ Tape

DIRECTIONS

* Define "domino effect" for the class: a situation in which one event causes a series of related events to happen, one after another. Ask students to share examples from their own lives. Maybe they get in trouble at home, lose their video game privileges, get angry at a younger sibling, and so on. Challenge

CC CONNECTION!

By delineating the cause-effect events, in a story, students must "analyze how and why individuals, events, and ideas develop and interact over the course of a text" (R.3).

students to provide examples from history (e.g., delineating and linking some events leading to the Revolutionary War or the Civil Rights Movement). Explain that they will encounter the domino effect in literature, too. Authors link events in a cause-and-effect way, usually to build the rising action.

* Have students work with a partner or in a small group of no more than three. Go over the assignment sheet. Ask them to start with a specific event in the text that is a catalyst for other events. It could be the event that introduces the climax and starts the rising action, or it could be an event that happens somewhere along the rising action. If you want to be sure that all the major events in the text are covered, assign different catalytic events to different groups—although they will most likely not choose the same event.

* After students write and attach the events to dominoes, give groups a chance to explain their events and thinking to the rest of the class.

* Line up the domino events in order and let them fall. If you assign specific events to groups, make a giant class line of dominoes and watch the whole plot line go down! If students choose their own starting event, see how the groups work with one another to put all the dominoes in order.

50 Common Core Reading Response Activities © 2014 by Marilyn Pryle, Scholastic Teaching Resources

Assignment: Domino Effect

1. Think of an event in the text that caused a series of other events to happen. Paraphrase it below, and then find where it happened in the text and write the **page number,** too.

_____

_____

_____

2. Now, think of at least four other events that happened because of this original event. Write them below, and include **page numbers** for each.

a. _____

_____

b. _____

_____

c. _____

_____

d. _____

_____

3. Write these five events, and their page numbers, on index cards. Write the first event on a card of a different color. If there is time, draw a picture of the event on the back of the card.

4. Tape each index card to a domino, and arrange the dominos in sequential order.

5. Knock down the dominoes!

Character Scrapbook

What It Is: A scrapbook of memories created by a character *(during and after reading)*

Use It With: Fiction, drama, autobiography

Make this activity as big or small as you like, or as you have time for. The goal is for students to demonstrate a deep understanding of a character by including quotations (said by the character, other characters, or a third-person narrator), traits, places, objects, and moments from the character's life, illustrated by pictures—everything you'd find in an actual scrapbook.

MATERIALS

✓ Assignment: Character Scrapbook for each student, p. 68

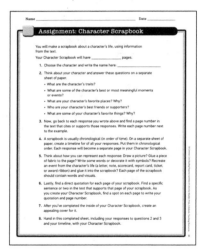

✓ Sample scrapbooks

✓ Sheets of white paper and construction paper for scrapbooks

✓ Markers, crayons, colored pencils

✓ Yarn or a stapler

✓ Tape and glue

✓ Any other stickers, letters, fabrics, and so on, that could be used as decorations

The structure of the text dictates whether this is a during- or post-reading activity: If a character's past isn't revealed until later in the story, then the scrapbook should be constructed afterward. A chronological layout works best here, like a real scrapbook one would make at home. For that reason, this activity is particularly useful for a character whose story is told in flashbacks; students can visually map out the character's life.

DIRECTIONS

* Explain the concept of a scrapbook to students, and show them at least one example.

* If the text is long and the scrapbooks would contain a large amount of information, pair or group students. Ask each pair or group to choose a character, or assign characters to ensure all of them will be represented in the scrapbook. On the board, write the minimum number of scrapbook pages and quotations from the text that each pair or group will contribute.

* Have students brainstorm ideas for the scrapbook on a separate sheet of paper. Encourage them to go back to the text to answer questions like those on the next page on a separate sheet of paper.

What are the character's traits?

What are some of the character's best or most meaningful moments or events?

What are the character's favorite places? Why?

Who are the character's best friends or supporters?

What are some of your character's favorite things? Why?

Students should find a quotation that answers the question and write the page number beside it.

* On another sheet of paper, students should create a timeline for the character, and arrange the events in the character's life in chronological order.

* Students should then think of a visual for each example. On the scrapbook page, they could draw a picture, glue a piece of fabric, write some words, or decorate it with symbols. Students could recreate something from the character's life (a letter, note, scorecard, report card, ticket, or an award).

* Have students create the scrapbook pages. Each page should have a topic, cited quotation, and at least one visual element. Remind students to have an appealing cover as well. They can staple or tie the pages together with yarn.

BUILD A RUBRIC
Process: Brainstorm and timeline
Minimum number of pages
Meaningful topic on each page
Cited quotation on each page
Interesting visual on each page
Appealing cover
Effort and creativity
Grammar, mechanics, spelling

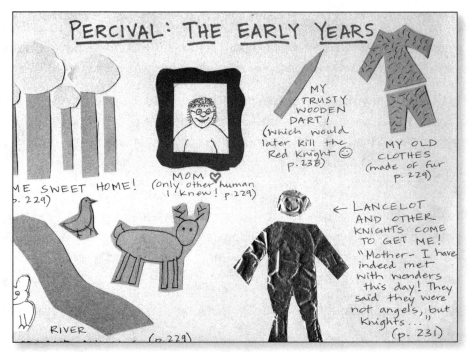

A page from a scrapbook for Percival from King Arthur and His Knights of the Round Table *(Green, 2008)*

Assignment: Character Scrapbook

You will make a scrapbook about a character's life, using information from the text.

Your Character Scrapbook will have _____ pages.

1. Choose the character and write the name here: _____

2. Think about your character and answer these questions on a separate sheet of paper.

   - What are the character's traits?

   - What are some of the character's best or most meaningful moments or events?

   - What are your character's favorite places? Why?

   - Who are your character's best friends or supporters?

   - What are some of your character's favorite things? Why?

3. Now, go back to each response you wrote above and find a page number in the text that cites or supports those responses. Write each page number next to the example.

4. A scrapbook is usually chronological (in order of time). On a separate sheet of paper, create a timeline for of all your responses. Put them in chronological order. Each response will become a separate page in your Character Scrapbook.

5. Think about how you can represent each response: Draw a picture? Glue a piece of fabric to the page? Write some words or decorate it with symbols? Recreate an event from the character's life (a letter, note, scorecard, report card, ticket, or award ribbon) and glue it into the scrapbook? Each page of the scrapbook should contain words and visuals.

6. Lastly, find a direct quotation for each page of your scrapbook. Find a specific sentence or two in the text that supports that page of your scrapbook. As you create your Character Scrapbook, find a spot on each page to write your quotation and page number.

7. After you've completed the inside of your Character Scrapbook, create an appealing cover for it.

8. Hand in this completed sheet, including your responses to questions 2 and 3 and your timeline, with your Character Scrapbook.

Character Facebook Page

What It Is: A character's Facebook page *(during or after reading)*

Use It With: Fiction, autobiography, drama

To create a Character Facebook page, students will need to know about the character's background: friends, hobbies, place of birth, school or work, major life events, and so on. The real fun, however, comes with the posts. The main character can post thoughts, and other characters can respond or just "like" the posts. Other characters can also post thoughts on the character's wall. It is this interaction between characters that reveals students' deeper comprehension of the text, and their ability to make inferences about characters and situations.

MATERIALS

✓ Facebook Page Brainstorming Sheet for each student, p. 71

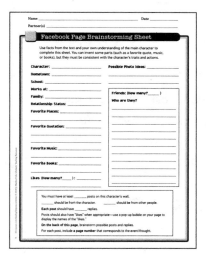

✓ Sheets of paper for drafting

✓ Sheets of white paper, posterboard, or butcher paper for final pages

✓ Markers, crayons, colored pencils

Note: On Facebook, clicking on a category like "Friends," "Likes," or "About" takes you to a new Web page; this can be replicated by having a sheet of paper for each Web page.

Overview: Pairs or small groups of three work best for this activity. Tailor the assignment to best meet the needs of your students. Here are two possibilities:

1. Give students a large poster with the categories in a Facebook layout; they will then fill in the information.

2. Assign an amount, such as "three Facebook pages," and let students figure out which categories to include and how to arrange them. To ensure that students are drawing inferences about the characters and events, require that at least one page consists of posts with replies. You can also require that posts be about a certain event in the text or specify the number of posts (e.g., five posts about events in the rising action and one post about the climax, with two replies for each post).

One feature that is difficult to replicate is the prevalence of pictures on Facebook—every friend, place, and "like" is usually accompanied by a picture. I tell students that they can be creative with illustrations, and if they become too frustrated, to use words only. If time permits, or if motivation is high, kids can print, cut and paste, or draw pictures. However, if that is too difficult or time-consuming, words will always suffice.

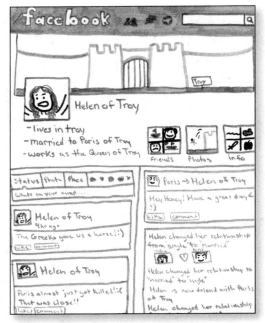

Student's Facebook page for Helen of Troy   "Likes" page for Helen of Troy Facebook page

DIRECTIONS

* Give an overview of Facebook and introduce the assignment.

* Have pairs or groups choose a character (or assign characters yourself) and then brainstorm elements to plan their Character Facebook pages.

* Ask students to do the following:

   • *Think of several photo ideas for their character*

   • *Brainstorm all of the character's "Friends"*

   • *Write several posts (from themselves or others) and replies, which other characters can "like" or respond to*

* Have students cite page numbers for all or some of their posts.

* Then tell students to transfer all the information to their final pages to create a finished product.

<table>
<tr><td colspan="1">BUILD A RUBRIC</td></tr>
<tr><td>Character background information (town, school, work, family, relationships)</td></tr>
<tr><td>Character favorites (places, quotes, music, books)</td></tr>
<tr><td>Likes</td></tr>
<tr><td>Picture of character</td></tr>
<tr><td>Minimum number of posts with page numbers</td></tr>
<tr><td>Minimum number of replies with page numbers</td></tr>
<tr><td>Creativity and effort</td></tr>
<tr><td>Grammar, mechanics, spelling</td></tr>
</table>

Facebook Page Brainstorming Sheet

Use facts from the text and your own understanding of the main character to complete this sheet. You can invent some parts (such as a favorite quote, music, or books), but they must be consistent with the character's traits and actions.

Character: _____

Hometown: _____

School: _____

Works at: _____

Family: _____

Relationship Status: _____

Favorite Places: _____
_____

Favorite Quotation: _____
_____
_____

Favorite Music: _____
_____

Favorite Books: _____
_____

Likes (How many?_____): _____
_____

Possible Photo Ideas: _____
_____
_____

Friends: (How many?_____)

Who are they?

_____
_____
_____
_____
_____
_____
_____
_____
_____
_____
_____

You must have at least _____ posts on this character's wall.

_____ should be from the character.   _____ should be from other people.

Each post should have _____ replies.

Posts should also have "likes" when appropriate—use a pop-up bubble on your page to display the names of the "likes."

On the back of this page, brainstorm possible posts and replies.

For each post, include **a page number** that corresponds to the event/thought.

50 Common Core Reading Response Activities © 2014 by Marilyn Pryle, Scholastic Teaching Resources

Chain of Events

What It Is: A paper chain with story events or points from an essay or steps in a procedure, and so on, linked together *(after reading)*

Use It With: Fiction and nonfiction

This activity involves students in choosing important events, summarizing and paraphrasing, citing, and recognizing the progression of events in a story or piece of nonfiction. It can be done with a chapter or an entire text, and it works best with partners or small groups so students can discuss and deliberate.

MATERIALS

✓ Assignment: Chain of Events for each student, p. 74

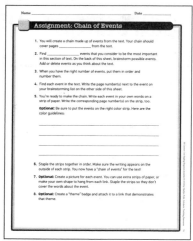

✓ Pre-cut strips (about 1/3 of a page lengthwise) of different-colored construction paper

✓ Stapler

✓ Sheets of paper for additional illustrations (optional)

✓ Markers

DIRECTIONS

* Give each pair or group ten strips of paper (or set another amount).

CC CONNECTION!

By linking together main events, students must explicitly understand the story (R.1) and analyze how events develop and interact (R.3).

---

* Ask pairs or groups to identify the ten most important events in the story or chapter and summarize each on a strip of paper, citing each with a page number.

* Have them staple the strips together to form a chain. The strips should be curved so the words are visible on the outside. Students now have a visual representation of how and when the events in the text are connected.

How to Display

The chain can be hung on a wall in a line or in a traditional plot-chart hill formation. You could even hang it from the ceiling! For a story with multiple plotlines, splay the plotlines out like tentacles, ensuring that the interconnections are visible.

Variations

Link Chains: For longer texts, assign different sections to each group. In the end, all the group's small chains will link together to form a large class chain.

Color Code: Color-code different parts of the story. The introduction could be blue, rising action could be orange, and the link that represents the climax could be red.

Split the Plot: A plot split into two or three storylines could be represented by having mini-chains diverge from the main chain.

50 Common Core Reading Response Activities © 2014 by Marilyn Pryle, Scholastic Teaching Resources

These mini-chains could also be on different-colored paper. Hang the chains on a wall so the various plot paths are visible.

Picture the Chain: Have students create a picture to go along with each link. The pictures could be drawn on a sheet of paper and stapled to each link so they hang down below the chain. These illustrations should not cover the words on the original link but provide a further visual below each plot point.

Create Theme Links: Have students make other hanging badges to represent the story's themes. A paper strip with a "T" could signify "theme," and below the "T," students could identify a theme. When a plot link touches upon a theme, the theme badge could be attached to dangle below it (or below the picture, if there is one).

A Step Further: Try It With Nonfiction

This activity can work with a variety of nonfiction forms, such as persuasive arguments, process essays, directions, and descriptive texts. Each idea can go on a link; links can be color-coded to represent theses, examples, reasons, steps, categories, introductions, conclusions, and so on. The chain can be arranged in a variety of ways depending on your text. You could have main ideas with supporting ideas dangling from them, or larger links designated as "Step #1," "Step #2," and so on, with the details of each step dangling sequentially below. Look at your text and its genre to determine which visual format would best aid student understanding. You can adapt the Assignment: Chain of Events sheet to work with a nonfiction text.

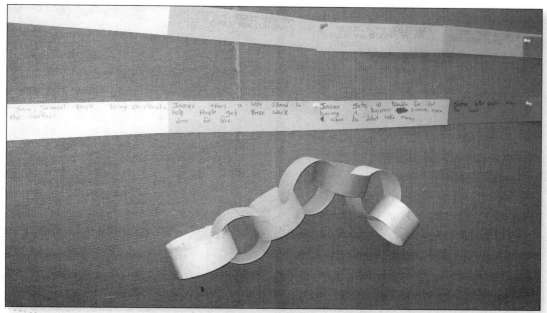

Color-coded student chains, shown unlinked and linked, for the short story "The Scribe" by Kristin Hunter (1995)

Assignment: Chain of Events

1. You will create a chain made up of events from the text. Your chain should cover pages _____ from the text.

2. Find _____ events that you consider to be the most important in this section of text. On the back of this sheet, brainstorm possible events. Add or delete events as you think about the text.

3. When you have the right number of events, put them in order and number them.

4. Find each event in the text. Write the page number(s) next to the event on your brainstorming list on the other side of this sheet.

5. You're ready to make the chain. Write each event in your own words on a strip of paper. Write the corresponding page number(s) on the strip, too.

   Optional: Be sure to put the events on the right color strip. Here are the color guidelines:

   _____

   _____

   _____

   _____

6. Staple the strips together in order. Make sure the writing appears on the outside of each strip. You now have a "chain of events" for the text!

7. **Optional:** Create a picture for each event. You can use extra strips of paper, or make your own shape to hang from each link. Staple the strips so they don't cover the words about the event.

8. **Optional:** Create a "theme" badge and attach it to a link that demonstrates that theme.

Interest Boards

What It Is: A reproduction of an interest board, such as a Pinterest page, belonging to a character *(during or after reading)*

Use It With: Fiction, autobiography, drama

Pinterest is basically an online scrapbook. It has no prescribed categories; the user creates his or her own categories, or "boards." These boards function like real-life bulletin boards on which anything—pictures, quotes, Web sites, recipes, books, and so on—can be "pinned." The more creative students get, the more they reveal their understanding of the character and events in the story.

MATERIALS

✓ Assignment: Interest Board for each student, p. 77

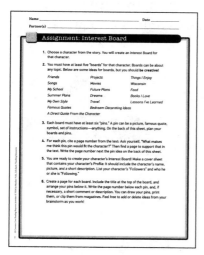

✓ Computer

✓ Sheets of paper for drafts

✓ Markers, crayons, colored pencils

✓ Magazines (optional)

DIRECTIONS

✱ Guide students on a tour of pre-selected boards on the Pinterest Web site (https://www.pinterest.com/).

CC CONNECTION!

By attaching page numbers to the pins, students will be "read[ing] closely to determine what the text says explicitly and to make . . . inferences" as well as citing "specific textual evidence" (R.1).

✱ Have pairs or small groups choose a character from the text and create a Pinterest page for him or her.

✱ Explain that each character must have a certain number of "boards." Board topics could pertain to just about anything, including the following:

Friends	*Projects*
Things I Enjoy	*Songs*
Movies	*Wisconsin*
My School	*Future Plans*
Bedroom	*Decorating Ideas*
Food	*Summer Plans*
Books I Love	*Dreams*
My Own Style	*Travel*
Famous Quotes	
Direct Quotes From Me (Character)	
Lessons I've Learned	

✱ Tell students that they must place a certain number of "pins" on each board and that for each pin, they must cite a page number from the text. Encourage them to be creative: A pin could be a picture, quotation, symbol, set of instructions—anything. Students should use one sheet of paper for each board, writing the title of each board at the top of the sheet of paper and arranging the

---

pins below. A board title could be clear and straightforward or quirky and fun. Some Pinterest users have whole sentences as board titles. As a fun challenge, require that one of the board titles be a direct quote from the character.

* Have students plan their boards and pins on draft paper.

* Tell students to start their final copies with a cover sheet representing the character's Profile. This should include the character's name, picture, and a short personal description. As with most social networking sites, Pinterest allows a user to follow and be followed, so students could list the character's "Followers" and those the character is "Following" on the cover sheet, too.

* Remind students to write page numbers below each pin on their final copies and, if they wish, a short comment or description as well. Pins can be drawn, printed, or

<table>
<tr><td colspan="1">BUILD A RUBRIC</td></tr>
<tr><td>Cover sheet with name, picture, description, followers/following</td></tr>
<tr><td>5 boards with titles</td></tr>
<tr><td>6 pins per board</td></tr>
<tr><td>Page number per pin</td></tr>
<tr><td>Grammar, spelling, mechanics</td></tr>
</table>

clipped from magazines. Students can add or delete pins as they work, as long as their final copy hits the required number.

Variation

A Simpler Interest Board: For a simpler variation, students could produce an Interest Board page about an entire story, creating boards for "Characters," "Theme," "Climax," and so on. On each board, they would pin pictures, quotes, and symbols to represent each category.

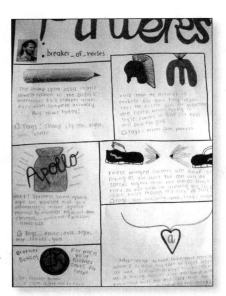

Interest Board for Hector from the Iliad (1998)

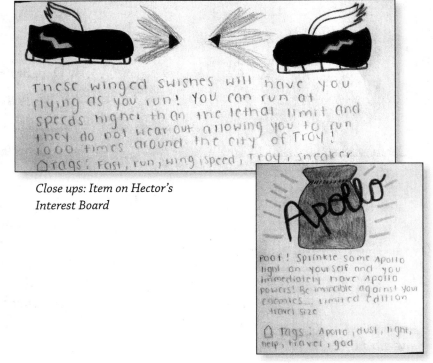

Close ups: Item on Hector's Interest Board

50 Common Core Reading Response Activities © 2014 by Marilyn Pryle, Scholastic Teaching Resources

Name _____ Date _____

Partner(s) _____

Assignment: Interest Board

1. Choose a character from the story. You will create an Interest Board for that character.

2. You must have at least five "boards" for that character. Boards can be about any topic. Below are some ideas for boards, but you should **be creative!**

Friends	*Projects*	*Things I Enjoy*
Songs	*Movies*	*Wisconsin*
My School	*Future Plans*	*Food*
Summer Plans	*Dreams*	*Books I Love*
My Own Style	*Travel*	*Lessons I've Learned*
Famous Quotes	*Bedroom Decorating Ideas*	
A Direct Quote From the Character		

3. Each board must have at least six "pins." A pin can be a picture, famous quote, symbol, set of instructions—anything. On the back of this sheet, plan your boards and pins.

4. For each pin, cite a page number from the text: Ask yourself, "What makes me think this pin would fit the character?" Then find a page to support that in the text. Write the page number next the pin idea on the back of this sheet.

5. You are ready to create your character's Interest Board! Make a cover sheet that contains your character's Profile: It should include the character's name, picture, and a short description. List your character's "Followers" and who he or she is "Following."

6. Create a page for each board. Include the title at the top of the board, and arrange your pins below it. Write the page number below each pin, and, if necessary, a short comment or description. You can draw your pins, print them, or clip them from magazines. Feel free to add or delete ideas from your brainstorm as you work!

50 Common Core Reading Response Activities © 2014 by Marilyn Pryle, Scholastic Teaching Resources

Create a Newspaper

What It Is: A newspaper about events in a text (*during and after reading*)

Use It With: Fiction, autobiography, drama

This activity is an oldie but goodie, and has even more potential with the technology available to us. Students can create a newspaper with a program like Publisher and print it out, or submit one to you online. It is best done as a during- or post-reading activity, when students can create stories, ads, obituaries, and wanted postings about the text. Pictures and cartoons enhance the writing. Over the years, I have assigned newspapers several times, and students always enjoy doing them.

MATERIALS

✓ Assignment: Create a Newspaper for each student, p. 80

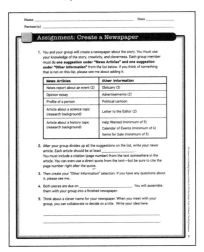

✓ A variety of newspapers

✓ Sheets of paper for drafts

✓ Sheets of paper for final copies

✓ Markers, crayons, colored pencils

✓ Computers (optional)

CC CONNECTION!

By writing factual reports, opinion essays, ads, wanted posts, obituaries, and so on, students are not only examining text and making inferences (R.1) but also summarizing key ideas (R.2) and analyzing interactions among characters and events R.3).

DIRECTIONS

* Tell students they will be producing their own newspaper based on people, places, and events in the text. Creating a newspaper is a large task, so have small groups of four or five students work together. Display the newspapers and introduce the parts they must incorporate, such as those shown in the box below:

ARTICLES	OTHER
• News Report About an Event	• Obituaries
• 2nd News Report About an Event	• Advertisements
• Opinion Essay	• Political Cartoon
• Profile of a Person	• Cartoon Strip
• Letter to the Editor	• Calendar of Events
• 2nd Letter to the Editor	• Help Wanted
• Science/History Article (research background)	• Items for Sale

* Explain to students that they will each write one "Article" and one "Other." Give groups time to divide up the work.

* Students should individually draft their articles and other pieces. You could require them to reference their information with page numbers from the text. For an even greater challenge, you could ask students to include and cite direct quotes in their articles. Citing page numbers will compel them to reread and pinpoint important parts of the text.

✻ If computers are available, students can type their articles. They can draw, write, or type their additional piece.

✻ When everyone's pieces are finalized, have each group work together to arrange them into a cohesive newspaper. This cutting and pasting can be done by hand or on a computer, with Publisher or another program. Remind students to think of a clever name for their newspaper.

How to Grade: You can give individual grades as well as a group grade. I usually give students a day or two to plan and start this in class, and then they are on their own to write and design their assigned sections. I may give them an additional day right before the due date to assemble their sections and print a final product.

BUILD A RUBRIC

Article reflects events
Page number with article
Article: Grammar, mechanics, spelling
"Other" piece reflects events
"Other" piece: grammar, mechanics, spelling
Effort, creativity
Overall product (group grade)

Newspaper generated from events in S. E. Hinton's
The Outsiders *(2012)*

Assignment: Create a Newspaper

1. You and your group will create a newspaper about the story. You must use your knowledge of the story, creativity, and cleverness. Each group member must do **one suggestion under "News Articles" and one suggestion under "Other Information"** from the list below. If you think of something that is not on this list, please see me about adding it.

News Articles	Other Information
News report about an event (2)	Obituary (3)
Opinion essay	Advertisements (2)
Profile of a person	Political cartoon
Article about a science topic (research background)	Letter to the Editor (2)
Article about a history topic (research background)	Help Wanted (minimum of 5) Calendar of Events (minimum of 6) Items for Sale (minimum of 5)

2. After your group divides up all the suggestions on the list, write your news article. Each article should be at least _____ .
You must include a citation (page number) from the text somewhere in the article. You can even use a direct quote from the text—but be sure to cite the page number right after the quote.

3. Then create your "Other Information" selection. If you have any questions about it, please see me.

4. Both pieces are due on _____ . You will assemble them with your group into a finished newspaper.

5. Think about a clever name for your newspaper. When you meet with your group, you can collaborate to decide on a title. Write your idea here:

_____

_____ .

Figurative Language Stations

What It Is: Stations around the room where students can explore figurative language (*before, during, or after reading*)

Use It With: Any text

By middle school, most students will be familiar with the basic forms of figurative language, and stations will get them up and moving around. Divide the class into four groups; at each station, they can split into pairs.

MATERIALS

✓ Figurative Language Station Directions for each station, p. 84

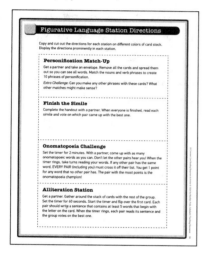

✓ Colored card stock
✓ Envelopes
✓ Scissors
✓ Tape or tacks

Grammar Bonus!

Use the nouns and verb phrases on the next page for a subject-verb refresher mini-lesson.

CC CONNECTION!

By finding quotations and organizing them thematically, students must "read closely" and "cite specific textual evidence" (R.1) and "analyze how two or more texts address similar themes" (R.9).

PERSONIFICATION MATCH-UP STATION

This activity for pairs is especially useful with ELL students, since it is done with a partner and requires conversation. Students work to match nouns with verb phrases to make a complete personified phrase. Ten examples appear on the next page; feel free to add more of your own, especially if you can find some in the text you're reading. Although the example phrases appear in matched form, that does not mean these matches are the only answers—with creative thinking, other matches are possible. The discussion during the activity is the most important aspect. For an extra challenge, students can make as many matches as possible after going through a first round of matches.

MATERIALS:

index cards, red and blue markers, envelopes

DIRECTIONS

* Copy each noun and verb phrase on the next page on an index card. You may want to make the nouns blue and the verbs red, if you intend to attach a grammar lesson to this activity. Make about five sets for the station, or as many you would need for a whole-class session.

the moon	looked down
the window	gaped
the flower	bowed its head
the leaves	danced in the air
the bee	hummed a summer song
the river	sang to the forest
the wind	kicked the loose door
the mountain	held snow on its shoulders
the fog	crept on silent feet
the tree	stretched its arms

* Shuffle each set of index cards and put them in an envelope.

* Have partners read and match the phrases in their envelope.

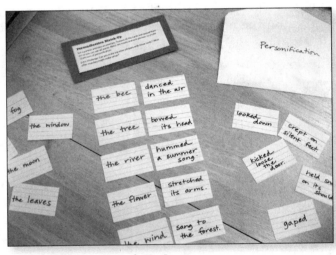

Personification Match-Up Station

FINISH THE SIMILE STATION

MATERIALS:

a pencil for each student, simile handout (see below)

This classic activity gives students the first half of a simile and asks them to finish the thought. At this station, the traveling group can split into partners to complete the task. When all the groups have finished, each group can read its answers aloud. Ask everyone to vote for the best simile in each round.

DIRECTIONS

* Create a handout with at least ten simile starters on it. Possibilities include:

as blue as	swift like a
as slim as	spiky like
as discordant as	yellow like
as fragrant as	sour like a
as slick as	peaceful like a

* Place handouts at the station. Have students complete the similes in pairs. Encourage them to avoid the easy responses and to use images from their own experiences. Remind them to be as specific as possible.

* Have pairs read the completed similes out loud. Ask the entire group to vote on the most interesting or entertaining examples for each simile.

ONOMATOPOEIA CHALLENGE STATION

MATERIALS:

paper and pencil for each student, a timer, posterboard, and markers (optional)

For this activity, students work in pairs. Set the timer for 2 minutes for each pair.

DIRECTIONS

* At the start of the timer, students generate as many onomatopoeic words as possible (*smack*, *bang*, *hiss*, and so on).

* When the timer goes off, partners stop writing and take turns reading their lists aloud.

 50 Common Core Reading Response Activities © 2014 by Marilyn Pryle, Scholastic Teaching Resources

* If any pairs have a matching word, everyone crosses that word off their list.

* Pairs get a point for each word they have that no other group has. The pair with the most points wins.

* To go a step further, have all pairs combine their words on a poster to display all year. This way, the concept stays alive in students' minds as they read.

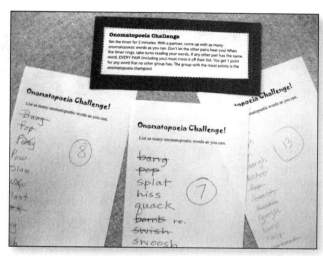

Onomatopoeia Challenge Station

ALLITERATION STATION

MATERIALS:

index cards, paper and pencil for each student, marker, a timer

DIRECTIONS

* Create a set of cards with a consonant on each card. Use all the consonants.

* Shuffle the cards. In the center of a table or desk, place the stack of cards face down.

* One of the partners flips over the first card, and the pair writes a sentence that contains at least five words that begin with that letter.

* Having pairs set a timer for 60 seconds will make this activity more exciting. When time is up, each pair reads its sentence. Then everyone votes on the winner for that round.

* * *

Although all these activities do not relate to a specific text, they prepare students more generally to recognize figurative language in their reading. And they're fun! Students enjoy moving around, working together, and thinking of silly phrases and sentences. On the next page are directions for each station to copy, cut, and post.

Figurative Language Station Directions

Copy and cut out the directions for each station on different colors of card stock. Display the directions prominently in each station.

Personification Match-Up

Get a partner and take an envelope. Remove all the cards and spread them out so you can see all words. Match the nouns and verb phrases to create 10 phrases of personification.

Extra Challenge: Can you make any other phrases with these cards? What other matches might make sense?

Finish the Simile

Complete the handout with a partner. When everyone is finished, read each simile and vote on which pair came up with the best one.

Onomatopoeia Challenge

Set the timer for 2 minutes. With a partner, come up with as many onomatopoeic words as you can. Don't let the other pairs hear you! When the timer rings, take turns reading your words. If any other pair has the same word, EVERY PAIR (including you) must cross it off their list. You get 1 point for any word that no other pair has. The pair with the most points is the onomatopoeia champion!

Alliteration Station

Get a partner. Gather around the stack of cards with the rest of the group. Set the timer for 60 seconds. Start the timer and flip over the first card. Each pair should write a sentence that contains at least 5 words that begin with the letter on the card. When the timer rings, each pair reads its sentence and the group votes on the best one.

50 Common Core Reading Response Activities © 2014 by Marilyn Pryle, Scholastic Teaching Resources

Mood Music

What It Is: An auditory activity to help students understand mood (*before, during, or after reading*)

Use It With: Fiction and nonfiction

An easy way to introduce mood is through music. Students love listening to music in class and anticipating what will come next in this activity.

MATERIALS
✓ A premade playlist (on MP3 or CD)
✓ Lined paper
✓ A reading sample for mood

DIRECTIONS
* Before class, make a playlist with snippets of various styles of music—for example, a colorful selection might include:

  A light, fun pop song

  A techno-sounding song

  An old-school rock song

  A light, classical flute piece

  A rousing gospel hymn

  A slow, sad pop song

  A jazz piece

  A weighty classical piece (like Beethoven's Symphony no. 5)

  You will only need about 20–30 seconds of each song, so decide which part of each song will have the most impact on mood.

* To introduce the concept of mood, ask students about the many different kinds of moods that people can experience and discuss their responses. Explain that music also has moods.

> ## CC CONNECTION!
> Exploring mood will help students "analyze how specific word choices shape meaning" in a text (R.4).

* Tell students that you are going to play sections of some music. They should listen and then write down what they think the mood of each section is.

* Play the first snippet and press "pause," so students have time to think and record their responses. If necessary, encourage them again to write a word for how the music feels. This first one may take a minute as students search for the right word.

* Repeat the process with each selection.

* Then replay the first selection and discuss students' responses.

* Point out that texts, like music, have moods. This can be a difficult concept to grasp. Most students agree that music gives them a certain feeling; that's why they like it. The tricky part is to get them to transfer that understanding to literature and informational texts. A discussion might go like this:

Ms. P.: So, everybody agrees that music gives you a feeling? (*Everyone nods.*) Can you give some examples about music that make you feel good? (*I take few answers.*) How about songs that make you feel angry, or sad? (*I take a few more answers.*) Okay. What is it about music that can make us feel happy or sad? What exactly creates that feeling in us?

Maria: A happy song is upbeat.

Ms. P.: Good! But what makes it upbeat?

Maria: From the beat—it's usually faster. And the drums or whatever is making the beat.

Ms. P.: Right! So the instruments can create mood. What else? Other examples?

Chris: For an angry song, the drums are hard, and the guitars are electric and harsh-sounding.

Anthony: Sad songs might be slow, like with a piano or something.

Ms. P.: Excellent. This is exactly it. (*I might take a few more answers before continuing.*)

Now, here's what I want you to think about (*I speak slowly here*). A text can do the same thing that the music does—it can make you feel an emotion, a *mood*. But a text doesn't do this with instruments. It does it with *words*. Write that down.

> A text creates
> <u>mood</u> with <u>words</u>.

At this point, have an example text ready to analyze for mood so that the class can try it out. When students approach a text not only understanding mood but also actively looking for it, they are more likely to correctly identify it.

50 Common Core Reading Response Activities © 2014 by Marilyn Pryle, Scholastic Teaching Resources

Word Alert! The Word Choice Web

What It Is: An organizer that examines an author's word choice *(during or after reading)*

Use It With: Fiction and nonfiction

Word Alert! is a handout I created to help students think deeply about a word and why the author used it. This activity cannot be done in isolation; it must be used during or after reading, since the main idea here is to examine a word in context. Note that on the handout on the next page I don't have a specific place for "definition"; the "synonym" space represents the definition, and students can use dictionaries if they need to. But the focus, once the word is understood, is to examine *why* the author chose that particular word instead of all the other words that were available. This is not so much a vocabulary exercise as it is a word-choice-questioning exercise.

MATERIALS

✓ One or more Word Alert! for each student, p. 88

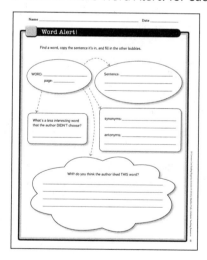

✓ Dictionaries (optional)

CC CONNECTION!

Intensely examining words in context will help students in determining "connotative . . . meanings" and analyzing how "word choices shape meaning or tone" (R.4).

Different Ways to Use Word Alert:

* Choose two words for students to work on.

* Have students choose their own words within a specific page range.

* Assign one word and have students choose the other.

* Specify that the words be verbs, adjectives, or adverbs.

* Have each student choose a word and then swap Word Alerts! with a partner. Each partner completes the other's page.

* Specify that the words be onomatopoeic, alliterative, or part of a simile or metaphor.

Different Ways to Review Word Alert:

* Have each student present one word to the class.

* Have students share words in pairs or small groups, and together choose the two most interesting words to present to the class.

* Create a vocabulary list from the class's words.

* Create a class glossary or word wall from the words.

* Have students illustrate one of the words and show its relation to the scene depicted.

* Create a Wordle with all of students' words (See "Create a Wordle" on p. 51.)

Name _____ Date _____

Word Alert!

Find a word, copy the sentence it's in, and fill in the other bubbles.

WORD: _____

page: _____

Sentence: _____
_____
_____

What's a *less interesting* word that the author DIDN'T choose?

_____

synonyms: _____
_____

antonyms: _____
_____

WHY do you think the author liked THIS word?

_____
_____
_____
_____

50 Common Core Reading Response Activities © 2014 by Marilyn Pryle, Scholastic Teaching Resources

Figurative Language Scavenger Hunt

What It Is: An organizer for identifying figurative language in a text (*during or after reading*)

Use It With: Fiction and nonfiction

Much like the Word Alert! web in the previous chapter, the aim of the Figurative Language Scavenger Hunt handout is to help students analyze an author's word choice— this time, with figurative language.

MATERIALS

✓ Figurative Language Scavenger Hunt! for each student, p. 90

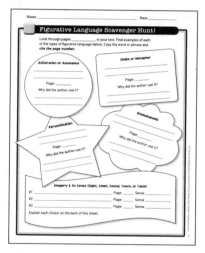

DIRECTIONS

* Emphasize to students that the figurative language in a piece of writing—similes, metaphors, personification, onomatopoeia, alliteration, and so on—isn't accidental; the author chooses these particular symbols or sounds in order to reinforce the mood, theme, or a plot point. For example, at one moment in a story, rain is falling. If the author wants to depict a safe, happy moment, he or she could use the phrase "rain fell like soft kisses." To suggest an

CC CONNECTION!

Students will be "determining . . . figurative meanings" and analyzing how words "shape meaning or tone" (R.4).

ominous moment, the author might say, "Rainclouds gathered like menacing ghosts." If the moment in question is a painful one, the author might use the personification of a phrase like "the drops pricked at his skin." It's important that students learn to recognize these choices and identify the meaning or mood the author is reinforcing.

* The Figurative Language Scavenger Hunt could be used with a few pages of text or an entire chapter. Students should skim the section for examples of figurative language, copy them, and cite the page number. This compels them to both reread for meaning and to apply the definitions of various figurative motifs (which they may have learned in isolation) to actual texts.

Partner Up!

Since this activity requires close rereading of larger passages, students can work together and divide the load.

Figurative Language Scavenger Hunt!

Look through pages _____ in your text. Find examples of each of the types of figurative language below. Copy the word or phrase and **cite the page number.**

Alliteration or Assonance

_____

_____

Page: _____

Why did the author use it?

_____

_____

Simile or Metaphor

_____

_____

Page: _____

Why did the author use it?

_____

_____

Personification

_____

_____

Page: _____

Why did the author use it?

_____

_____

Onomatopoeia

_____

_____

Page: _____

Why did the author use it?

_____

_____

Imagery & Its Sense (Sight, Smell, Sound, Touch, or Taste)

#1 _____ Page: _____ Sense _____

#2 _____ Page: _____ Sense _____

#3 _____ Page: _____ Sense _____

Explain each choice on the back of this sheet.

Tone Charades

What It Is: A game to help students identify different tones (*before, during, or after reading*)

Use It With: Fiction and nonfiction

Tone can be a difficult concept to grasp for middle school students. The "Mood Music" activity (page 85) demonstrated, via music, that mood comes from the outside in. With Tone Charades, students create the feeling within and send it out. They often enjoy this activity and carry it out with a lot of giggling, but by the end, they completely understand that tone affects meaning.

MATERIALS

✓ Tone Cards and Sentence Cards for each group, p. 93

✓ Index cards and marker (optional, if you want to create your own Tone Cards and Sentence Cards)

✓ A reading sample

DIRECTIONS

* Cut out a set of Tone Cards for each group, or create your own sets of cards. Label the back of each Tone Card with the word "Tone" or a "T."

* Cut out a set of Sentence Cards for each group, or create your own sets of cards with four or five sentences on each card. Label the backs of each Sentence Card with the word "Sentence" or an "S."

* Introduce the concept of tone with an easy, real-life example: Ask students if anyone has ever told them, "Don't take that tone with me!" This usually inspires an interesting discussion. Guide students to see that tone involves the feeling behind words.

* Form groups of four to six students. Tell them that they are going to play a game called "Tone Charades." Give each group a stack of Tone Cards, and a stack of Sentence Cards, both facedown.

* Have each group turn over its first Sentence Card.

* The first player should turn over a Tone Card, without showing it to the other players. That player should then say the sentence using the tone written on the card.

* The other players have to guess what the tone is. When they succeed in identifying the tone, the second player takes a Tone Card and repeats the same sentence in that tone. Everyone guesses what that tone is.

* When all the players have expressed a tone with the first sentence, have the group shuffle all the Tone Cards, flip over the next Sentence Card, and repeat the game.

It helps to start the activity with an easy example. Here's how it usually goes in my class:

Ms. P.: Today, we're going to talk about tone in literature. But first, we'll talk about it in real life. Has anyone ever told you, "Don't take that tone with me"?

(Hands invariably go up.)

Brian: Once my mom said it. I was saying how much I love when she tells me to clean my room. That she was the best mom ever.

Ms. P.: But those sound like nice things to say.

Brian: No, I was being sarcastic!

Ms. P.: Oh, so it was the *way* you said it that upset your mom.

Brian: Yes.

Ms. P.: This is what tone is. It's the *feeling* behind the words. And tone can have a lot of meaning, can't it? *(Students nod.)* Okay, that's what we're going to practice first. You're going to break up into groups of four or five, and I'm going to give each group an envelope. You'll read aloud each sentence in the envelope in a specific tone, and the rest of the group will try to guess what the tone it.

A Step Further: Take It to the Text

The most important step comes after the game, when you help students transfer their understanding to an actual text. Ask students how they figured out which tone their classmates were using. Then explain that an author can do the same with words. Even though we can't physically hear an author's voice, his or her words, images, and symbols communicate the tone of a text. Immediately have students examine the current text (or another example you've chosen) for tone in order to anchor this idea in their minds. Here's an example from my classroom:

Ms. P.: Okay, did you enjoy that? Was it easy to figure out the tones?

Amiee: Yes, it was funny. The person's voice changed each time. It helped to see that person's face, too.

Ms. P.: Right. Now, with a text, it's different—you can't see the author's face or hear his or her voice. But we can still tell how the author *feels*, can't we? Don't you think you can sometimes tell when an author—not a character, but the author—is angry or happy or sarcastic? How can we tell, if we can't see the author?

Declan: You can just tell when you read it, in the words.

Ms. P.: Yes! It's in the words. The author chooses words, images, and symbols to convey tone. Let's look at an example.

At this point, we turn to our current text, or if we are between texts, I give a short piece of writing for students to examine. They can work in pairs to identify the tone of the reading, and then pick out words, phrases, and images (I usually assign three to five) that create that tone. Students list these in their notebooks and prepare to discuss their findings.

50 Common Core Reading Response Activities © 2014 by Marilyn Pryle, Scholastic Teaching Resources

Tone Cards and Sentence Cards

Tone Cards

angry	excited
afraid	joyful
confused	hopeful

Sentence Cards

The circus is coming to town.	Your cell phone is ringing.
There are no more #2 pencils.	This snack is making me thirsty.

50 Common Core Reading Response Activities © 2014 by Marilyn Pryle, Scholastic Teaching Resources

Dig the Dialect, Man!

What It Is: A rewriting of text in a new dialect *(during or after reading)*

Use It With: Fiction and nonfiction

This activity is especially effective if you choose a text that is already in a certain dialect; for example, Shakespearean English sounds really funny in an urban New York dialect. *One caution:* You must monitor students to ensure that they do not insult a group through the use of its dialect.

DIRECTIONS

Check for text comprehension while exploring the notion of dialect by having students rewrite a section of text in a different dialect. Emphasize that they must reread the text closely in order to fully understand its meaning and "translate" it into another dialect.

Some examples of dialect include:

Your city's dialect	*Elizabethan English*
U.S. East Coast (New York, Boston)	*Colonial American English*
U.S. Southern	*Modern British English*
U.S. Midwestern (Chicago)	*American English in 1960s*
U.S. West Coast	*Canadian English*
American Old West (cowboy)	*Australian English*

Tip: To help students work with another dialect, Google vocabulary in that dialect and make a handout they can draw from.

> ### CC CONNECTION!
> By examining and changing the dialect in a text, students must "interpret words and phrases" and determine "connotative . . . meaning" (R.4).

Variations

Include Fictional and Fun Dialects: If students are having trouble writing in "real-life" dialects, give them the option of using their favorite books and movies. They could rewrite text in a *Star Wars* dialect, a *Star Trek* dialect, a *Harry Potter* dialect, or a *Lord of the Rings* dialect. They could write in a pirate dialect, or a "valley girl" dialect. The poem below is Emily Dickinson's "I'm Nobody! Who Are You?" (1960) rewritten in the voice of Yoda from *Star Wars*.

> ### "I'M NOBODY! YOU, WHO ARE?"
> **by Yoda**
>
> Nobody I am; You, who are?
> Nobody, you are? Too, you are?
> Pair of us there is! Tell not!
> Banish us, they would. Banish, know you.
>
> Somebody being, dreary is.
> Public, somebody is. Frog-like, yes.
> Livelong day name telling, yes.
> To a bog admiring.

Assign the Dialects of Historic Figures: Make this a cross-curricular activity by asking students to rewrite the text in the voice of a historic figure. For instance, you might suggest that students use the voice of Ben Franklin or Martin Luther King, Jr. Students could imitate their dialects as well as weave in some of these people's ideas if they match the ideas in the text.

50 Common Core Reading Response Activities © 2014 by Marilyn Pryle, Scholastic Teaching Resources

Text Puzzle

What It Is: An activity in which students reorder jumbled strips of text *(before reading)*

Use It With: Fiction and nonfiction

This activity helps students see how the parts of a text come together to form the whole. They must physically rearrange jumbled strips of text into the original order. Shorter nonfiction (persuasion, process, comparison, and so on), speeches, shorter narratives, poetry, and soliloquies work especially well here.

MATERIALS
✓ Text puzzle strips (see below)
✓ Scissors
✓ Envelopes
✓ Overhead projector

DIRECTIONS

* Select a portion of text. Cut and paste it into a word processing document.

* Divide the text into logical parts: main ideas, turns of argument, sequential steps, or examples. The writing itself will determine how it should be separated; for example, a persuasive essay could be divided into introduction, reasons, and conclusions, and for a further challenge, each example could also be extracted from its section, so students must figure out which main line of reasoning it supports. Most poems and soliloquies build upon examples and reasoning, too, arriving at some conclusion at the end. Narratives are usually sequential, with text clues given for flashbacks, so students should be able to figure out their progress.

* Reformat the parts so that spacing and paragraphing don't give away their location in the complete work. Otherwise, students

> ### CC CONNECTION!
> In recreating the order of a text, students must "analyze the structure of texts" and how the specific parts "relate to each other and the whole" (R.5).

will reconstruct the piece based merely on how the physical page fits together, not on the author's intention and progression of thought. Backspace tabbed topic sentences; drag middle-paragraph sentences back to the left margin. Line breaks in poetry could remain intact, but if you do decide to break a line, drag it back to the left margin as well.

* Cut the parts into separate strips. Shuffle the strips and put them into envelopes. You can label the envelope with the title or, if it is part of a longer work, with a label that will help students frame the piece in their minds, such as "Brutus's Soliloquy" or "Catherine's Letter."

* Have partners read all the strips, determine each idea's function, and arrange the ideas in the author's original order based on logic, transition words, emphasis, and so on.

The beauty of this activity lies in the fact that even if students don't correctly figure out the original layout, they have put themselves in the mind of the author, nonetheless, by trying to guess the author's purpose and logic. They have also used prior knowledge about transition words and how examples support reasoning. To finish the activity, put the original on your projector and read it with the whole class. Student interest will be high, not only because they want to see if they got it "right," but also because in the process they have, in a way, become co-authors of the piece.

The Hot Dog Cart

What It Is: A multiple retelling of a story from different points of view (*before, during, or after reading*)

Use It With: Fiction and nonfiction

This fun exercise gets students thinking about point of view before they even read a text.

MATERIALS

✓ Sheets of lined paper

✓ Copy of "The Hot Dog Cart" for each student, p. 97

The Hot Dog Cart
One day, a boy is walking his dog down a city street. It is a peaceful, sunny midday, and many people are about. Suddenly, the dog spots a hot dog vendor on the street corner, and without warning, snaps free of his leash and bolts for the cart. The dog jumps on the cart, tackling the vendor in the process, and the cart rolls into the street where it hits a convertible, launching the dog and several hot dogs into the driver's lap. The driver, a businessman, brakes to a halt, and the car behind him, driven by a teenager, rear-ends him. No one is hurt, but all traffic stops amid alarms and sirens.

DIRECTIONS

* Tell "The Hot Dog Cart" story on the next page to students. You may want to draw a diagram of the story on the board as you go. It's good practice to have students listen to the story and retell it from memory, but you can give them a handout for reference.

* Ask students to tell you which point of view the story was told from (third person).

* Put students into small groups and randomly assign one of the following characters to each group:

  boy, teenager, police officer, vendor, elderly bystander, businessman, dog

* Instruct students to rewrite the story from the first-person perspective of their assigned character. They should stick with the basic plotline, but invent any other details, feelings, or dialect appropriate to their

narrator. (They can also choose the gender of the gender-neutral characters.) You might want to set a minimum length for the story to ensure that students give it sufficient additional thought. They should give their version of the story a new title that is fitting to their narrator.

* Have each group read its version to the class. The differences in perspective will be apparent!

* As a closing exercise, ask the whole class the following question:

  How does the choice of narrator affect a text?

  Students should be able to come up with several answers, not only about what is gained from a particular narrator but also about what is lost. Remind students that as they read, they should always ask themselves why the author chose that particular narrator to tell the story. You could even make a poster like the one in the box below to prompt students to always examine an author's choices.

Consider the Narrator!

1. Why did the author choose this narrator?

2. What special information does this narrator give us?

3. What do we miss out on knowing because of this narrator?

The Hot Dog Cart

One day, a boy is walking his dog down a city street. It is a peaceful, sunny midday, and many people are about. Suddenly, the dog spots a hot dog vendor on the street corner, and without warning, snaps free of his leash and bolts for the cart. The dog jumps on the cart, tackling the vendor in the process, and the cart rolls into the street where it hits a convertible, launching the dog and several hot dogs into the driver's lap. The driver, a businessman, brakes to a halt, and the car behind him, driven by a teenager, rear-ends him. No one is hurt, but all traffic stops amid alarms and sirens.

How's the View?

What It Is: A web map of an author's point of view, purpose, and tone *(before, during, and after reading)*

Use It With: Persuasive nonfiction

The How's the View? web ties together point of view, purpose, tone, and genre. It also gets students to recognize audience and opposing points of view in a text, and asks them to engage in the topic by voicing their own views.

MATERIALS

✓ How's the View? web for each student, p. 99

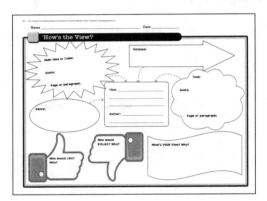

DIRECTIONS

* After reading aloud a persuasive text, give students the How's the View? web.

* On the board, list several possible choices students can use with both the "Genre" and "Purpose" bubbles. Options are shown in the boxes below.

Giving students additional options will guide them to go deeper, instead of simply writing "Persuasive Essay" for "Genre" and "To persuade" for "Purpose."

GENRE

- Letter to the Editor
- Open Letter (for public to read)
- Book/Music/Arts Review
- Op-Ed Essay
- Social Action Letter (to a politician or company)
- Online Product Review
- Speech

PURPOSE

- To persuade
- To entertain
- To inform
- To compare

How's the View?

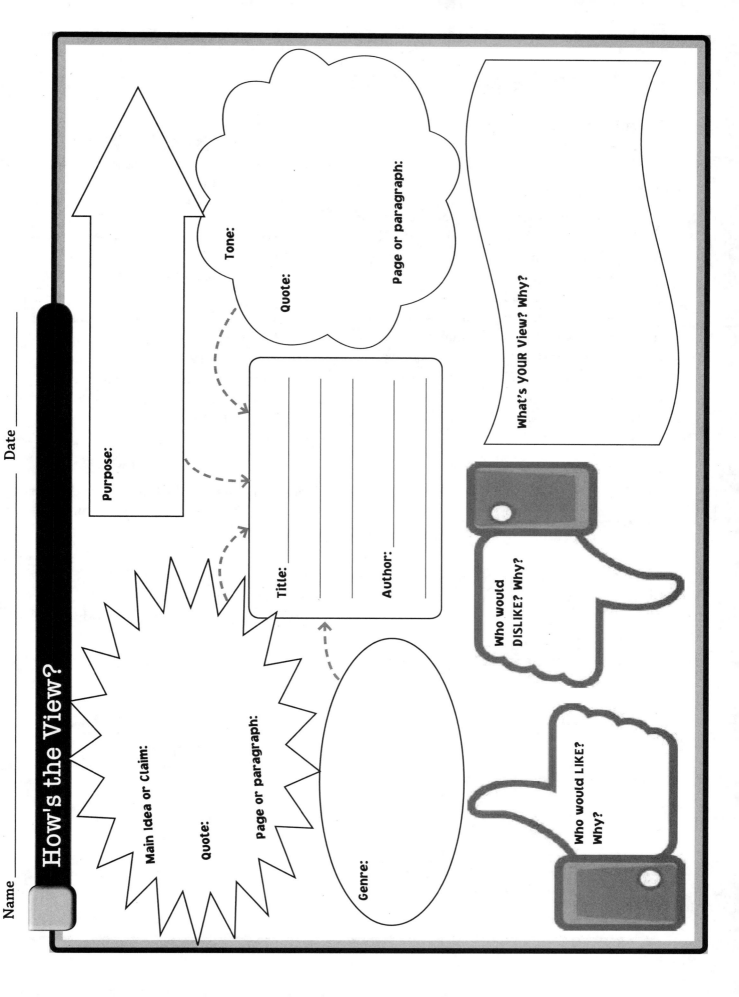

Purpose:

Tone:
Quote:
Page or paragraph:

What's YOUR View? Why?

Title: _____
_____
_____
Author: _____

Main Idea or Claim:
Quote:
Page or paragraph:

Genre:

Who would DISLIKE? Why?

Who would LIKE? Why?

Create a Mockumentary

What It Is: A video recreating a text, interspersed with character interviews (*during or after reading*)

Use It With: Fiction, autobiography, drama

In creating a "mockumentary" (like the popular television show, *The Office*, students not only reenact the events in the text, but they also give insight into the characters' real feelings, motivations, and reactions.

I love giving this assignment: the kids have fun, and I can measure their comprehension. Students' enjoyment of the mockumentary process ensures that they will remember the story longer than if they had written a paper or taken a test about it.

MATERIALS

✓ Assignment: Mockumentary for each group, p. 101

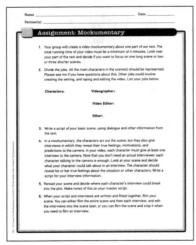

✓ Equipment for videotaping and playing mockumentaries

DIRECTIONS

* Form groups of five or six. Explain the concept of the mockumentary. You might introduce it like this: *In this mockumentary, the plot is acted out, but it's interrupted by*

interviews with individual characters who reveal their true feelings about an incident, the relationships of the people involved, random musings, and so on. During these interviews, you must remain in character, and use direct information and inferences about the text to be able to speak as the character.

* Go over the assignment sheet with students.

* Have groups choose which section of the text they want to reenact, or assign sections to ensure that the entire story will be portrayed in the mockumentary.

* After rehearsing, groups are ready to film their scripts. (This can be noisy, so you may want to let students film in the hall or outside of school.)

* Set aside class time to screen all the mockumentaries. After the viewing, focus discussion on point of view. After seeing all the characters' true feelings, ask students, "Would this story have been different with a different narrator? How?"

Assignment: Mockumentary

1. Your group will create a video mockumentary about one part of our text. The total running time of your video must be a minimum of 6 minutes. Look over your part of the text and decide if you want to focus on one long scene or two or three shorter scenes.

2. Divide the jobs. All the main characters in the scene(s) should be represented. Please see me if you have questions about this. Other jobs could involve creating the setting, and taping and editing the video. List your jobs below:

   Characters: **Videographer:**

                            Video Editor:

                            Other:

3. Write a script of your basic scene, using dialogue and other information from the text.

4. In a mockumentary, the characters act out the scene, but they also give interviews in which they reveal their true feelings, motivations, and predictions to the camera. In your video, each character must give at least one interview to the camera. Note that you don't need an actual interviewer; each character talking to the camera is enough. Look at your scene and decide what your character could talk about in an interview. The character should reveal his or her true feelings about the situation or other characters. Write a script for your interview information.

5. Reread your scene and decide where each character's interview could break into the plot. Make notes of this on your master script.

6. When your script and interviews are written and fitted together, film your scene. You can either film the entire scene and then each interview, and edit the interviews into the scene later, or you can film the scene and stop it when you need to film an interview.

Genre Recipes

What It Is: A written recipe for a specific genre *(during or after reading)*

Use It With: Any genre

After reading a specific genre or subgenre, you can have students write a "recipe" for that genre. They must ask themselves which "ingredients" make up this particular genre. What must authors use and combine to write in this genre? Students must consider the structure, qualities, and characteristics of a particular genre, and the skills required to create it, as well as the appropriate combination of each. In doing so, they must analyze the structure of the genre along with the author's intent.

MATERIALS

✓ Assignment: Genre Recipe for each student, p. 103

✓ Genre Recipe for each pair or group, p. 104

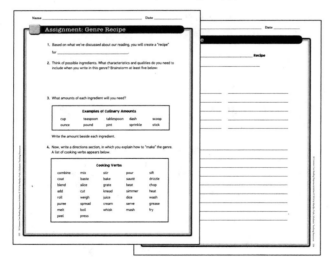

DIRECTIONS

* Assign a subgenre—preferably the one you've just read or are in the midst of reading—to partners or small groups. The more specific you can be in naming the subgenre, the better; for example, instead

---

CC CONNECTION!

By creating "recipes" for genres, students must "analyze the structure of texts" (R.5) and "assess how . . . purpose shapes the . . . style of a text" (R.6).

of fiction, specify science fiction; instead of poetry, specify limerick; instead of nonfiction article, specify letter to the editor. Students will have to explore the nuances of each subgenre and go deeper into considerations of structure, characteristics, and purpose.

* Go over the assignment sheet with students.

* Have students write the recipe for the subgenre. They should have an "Ingredients" section, listing the ingredients and their amounts, and a "Directions" section, explaining how to combine and transform the ingredients into a finished product.

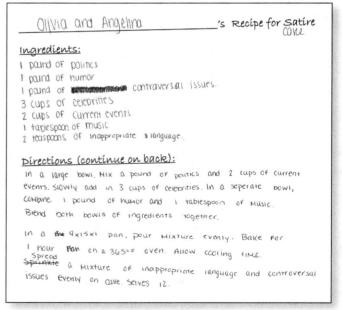

Sample Genre Recipe for a satire

---

50 Common Core Reading Response Activities © 2014 by Marilyn Pryle, Scholastic Teaching Resources

Assignment: Genre Recipe

1. Based on what we've discussed about our reading, you will create a "recipe"

   for _____.

2. Think of possible ingredients. What characteristics and qualities do you need to include when you write in this genre? Brainstorm at least five below:

3. What amounts of each ingredient will you need?

Examples of Culinary Amounts				
cup	teaspoon	tablespoon	dash	scoop
ounce	pound	pint	sprinkle	stick

   Write the amount beside each ingredient.

4. Now, write a directions section, in which you explain how to "make" the genre. A list of cooking verbs appears below.

Cooking Verbs				
combine	mix	stir	pour	sift
coat	baste	bake	sauté	drizzle
blend	slice	grate	beat	chop
add	cut	knead	simmer	heat
roll	weigh	juice	dice	wash
puree	spread	cream	serve	grease
melt	boil	whisk	mash	fry
peel	press			

Genre Recipe

_____ **Recipe**

for _____

Ingredients:

_____   _____

_____   _____

_____   _____

_____   _____

_____   _____

Directions:

_____

_____

_____

_____

_____

_____

_____

_____

_____

_____

Break Out From the Text

What It Is: Using additional nonprint material to complement text *(before, during, or after reading)*

Use It With: Fiction and nonfiction

We all know and love a quality film adaptation of the text we are reading in class. However, sometimes we can't find one, or if we do, we might not have three class days to spend watching it. In this activity, I suggest ways of incorporating audio and visual material to complement the texts you're reading.

MATERIALS

✓ Digital resources (see below)

✓ Break Out From the Text chart for each student, p. 107

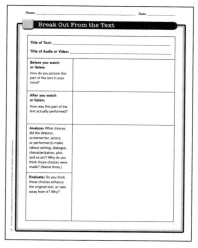

abound. On http://www.pbs.org, for example, you can find a video clip of Robert Frost reading "Stopping by Woods on a Snowy Evening." The Academy of American Poets Web site (http://www.poets.org) has a recording of the contemporary poet Galway Kinnell reading Emily Dickinson's "The Soul Selects Her Own Society."

Find historical speeches online: This can be done whether you are reading the speech itself or a story that takes place in the same historical time period. For example, if your class is reading Karen Hesse's *Out of the Dust* (1997), you could play "FDR's Fireside Chat on the Drought and the Dust Bowl" on http://www.OutoftheDust.history.com.

Find an audio recording of drama: Drama is meant to be seen and heard, so why do we make kids read it only? This is especially important for Shakespeare's work, which comes alive in the mouths of actors and becomes magically accessible to students when they can hear the actors' tones and inflections. Most plays have an audio version on http://www.amazon.com; some are free online.

Find a clip that parodies a scene from the story: This might take some searching, but parodies exist, especially of the classics. I love to show the song "Find Your Grail" from the Broadway show *Spamalot* when we read King Arthur. I found the clip on YouTube,

In addition to finding a film adaptation of a novel, you can also do the following:

Find a scene from a text or a film: YouTube is especially helpful here. Analyzing even one scene will hook students and provide a springboard for discussion.

Find audio recordings of poems online: Recordings of poems, whether by the original authors or other readers,

since the song had been performed at the Tony Awards. Of course, I could never show my class the entire movie *Monty Python and the Holy Grail*, which *Spamalot* is based on, but one clip from the Broadway adaptation was appropriate and enjoyable, and prompted some fruitful discussion. See what you can find!

Use an infographic: Whatever you're reading about probably has a related infographic available online. For example, if you're reading *Fever 1793* (Anderson, 2000), you can search "yellow fever infographic" and view several infographics about yellow fever and other historical pandemics. Infographics are creative graphs, flow charts, or diagrams of any kind that use engaging visuals to communicate information. Analyzing infographics both supplements the text with new information and gives students practice in dissecting visual media.

A Step Further: Create an Infographic

Once students are comfortable with reading and examining a large number of infographics, have them partner up and create their own, based on the text. Tell students to think about anything in the text that can be measured or graphed. This can be factual information (like the number of ships sent to Troy) or inferred (like the amount of rage each character has). Then have students draw this information in some form of graph or visual. Some examples are shown below.

* * *

Distribute and discuss the Break Out From the Text chart to help students gather their thoughts about a video or an audio presentation. You might have to give students examples, especially in the "Analyze" row, to help them understand that a movie director constantly makes choices about setting, characterization, dialogue, plot, and so on.

A student-generated infographic comparing the power of each god in The Iliad *(1998)*

A student-generated infographic comparing Homer's "1,000 ships" to the U. S. Navy

50 Common Core Reading Response Activities © 2014 by Marilyn Pryle, Scholastic Teaching Resources

Break Out From the Text

Title of Text: _____

Title of Audio or Video: _____

Before you watch or listen: How do you picture this part of the text in your mind?	
After you watch or listen: How was this part of the text actually performed?	
Analyze: What choices did the director, screenwriter, actors, or performer(s) make (about setting, dialogue, characterization, plot, and so on)? Why do you think those choices were made? (Name three.)	
Evaluate: Do you think these choices enhance the original text, or take away from it? Why?	

Experiment With Emphasis

What It Is: A group speaking activity focusing on vocal emphasis *(before, during, or after reading)*

Use It With: Fiction and nonfiction

This activity works well with a single important sentence from a text. These are easier to find in a speech, soliloquy, or poem, but can also be found in an article, a short story, or even a novel.

MATERIALS

✓ A set of sentences (see sample below) for each group

✓ An envelope for each group

DIRECTIONS

* After you find a pivotal or thematic line in a text, print it out several times (you should be able to fit about six on a sheet of paper) and then cut apart the lines. Underline a different word in each line—it can be any word, but choose your words by testing out the emphasis yourself first. Below is an example with John F. Kennedy's famous line, "Ask not

what your country can do for you; ask what you can do for your country."

* Before having students try the activity, set it up by tapping into their prior knowledge about emphasis. Ask what it means to emphasize a word when speaking. Use an easy example like the following sentence: *On Thursday, I happily chose to go to the movies.* Write it on the board and tell students to say it silently to themselves. Then underline the word *Thursday* and ask someone to stress this word as he or she says the sentence. Discuss whether this emphasis changes the meaning of the sentence and how it does. Then after erasing the line under *Thursday* and underlining *I*, ask another student to

---

<u>Ask</u> not what your country can do for you; <u>ask</u> what you can do for your country.

Ask <u>not</u> what your country can do for you; ask what you can do for your country.

Ask not what your <u>country</u> can do for you; ask what you can do for your country.

Ask not what your country can do for you; ask what you can do for <u>your</u> country.

Ask not what your country can <u>do</u> for you; ask what you can do for your country.

Ask not <u>what</u> your country can do for you; ask what you can do for your country.

---

read aloud the sentence, and the class to interpret any change in meaning. Repeat with *happily*, *chose*, and *movies*, and see what changes in meaning students hear. Ask if the tone of the sentence changes as well—depending on how one emphasizes *happily*, for instance, the tone could be sarcastic. Explain that we constantly use emphasis to convey our meaning.

* Put students in groups of five or six, and give each group an envelope that contains six versions of the same sentence with different words underlined for emphasis.

* Each student should take a sentence and read it, putting a heavy emphasis on the underlined word. Encourage them to really exaggerate the emphasis on the underlined word.

* After each sentence version is read, students should discuss the following questions:

How does the emphasized word shape or change the meaning of the sentence?

How does the emphasis shape the tone of the sentence?

* After groups discuss these questions, review the questions and responses as a whole class. As an additional discussion, you can ask students what cues writers use to indicate emphasis (i.e., italics, underlining, or all capitals).

* If you have a recording of the text—a video or an audio of the original speech or poem, for example, or a professional reading of the drama—play it for students after the discussion. If the recording is by the original author, students can hear the words he or she chose to emphasize. If no original exists but other renderings are available (as with Shakespeare's plays), you could present multiple interpretations and discuss the choices each performer made. By helping students tune in to how words can work when spoken aloud, they will gain insight into authors' styles and purposes.

Use Parodies!

What It Is: A humorous reenactment or rewrite of an original work *(after reading)*

Use It With: Fiction and nonfiction

MATERIALS

✓ A parody of a class text

Try to find a parody of the text you are reading in class. A parody might exist in print or in the form of a video or an audio clip. It might target the plot or characters, but it might also poke fun at the theme or style. With poetry, a parody might imitate the wording, tone, or style of the author. This can be difficult with newer works, but many print and film parodies exist for the classics. The ability to appreciate a parody reflects a sophisticated understanding of the original. Plus, students love any humorous deviation from the text! Often, I find that they remember a parody more clearly than the original work. And—whether they realize it or not—students are quite familiar with parody already: The cartoons and other television shows they grow up with are rife with parody.

DIRECTIONS

* Do a print and/or an online search of your text and see what comes up. Even if you can only find a short snippet of a parody, that could be enough to introduce the concept and reinforce the meaning of the original work.

* Allow time for students to watch or read the parody, and discuss in small groups what's happening in it. To help students better understand parody, ask the following questions (you may want to write them on the board or create a handout):

What aspects of the original text does the parody poke fun at? Think of as many as possible.

How does the parody make fun of these aspects?

What message do you think the creators of the parody are trying to send?

Did you think the parody was effective? Why or why not?

What is one more thing from the original text that you could add to the parody? Describe it.

Follow-Up Idea: Create a Genre Recipe!

After students have analyzed a parody, they can create a "Recipe for Parody" (see page 102). This will help them put the elements of parody into words.

A Step Further: Create a Parody

Students can choose a different part of the text, or another poem by the same author, and try creating their own parodies of it. Depending on the original, they may want to parody the style, characters, plot, or all three. Students may produce a written parody or work in groups to act it out. Whatever the form, students demonstrate an in-depth understanding of the original when they write their own parodies. Below are some ideas for parody assignments:

- Write a poem using the same diction and rhyme scheme as the original, but poke fun at the content.

- Reenact a scene from the story, but give a funny twist on the events.

- Put a character from the story in a different setting (time or place) and write a scene about it.

Another Follow-Up Idea: Doh!

The creators of *The Simpsons* produced a parody of Homer's *Odyssey* called "The Odyssey of Homer (Simpson)." This episode appeared in the third episode of the first season.

- Reenact a scene from the story, but give the characters opposite traits and qualities.

- Have characters interviewed in a modern talk-show format, or put characters in a reality-TV show situation.

Report Card

What It Is: An evaluation of an author's reasoning (*after reading*)

Use It With: Persuasive nonfiction

In this activity, students must figure out an author's argument and reasoning, and evaluate his or her claims.

MATERIALS

✓ Report Card for each student, p. 113

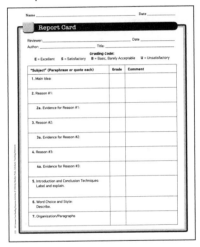

✓ Comment sheet, photocopied

DIRECTIONS

* After reading a persuasive article, explain to students that they will "grade" the author

on how effective the article was. Emphasize that just because something is published doesn't mean it's perfect! Some sections of the text might be better than others, or the whole piece might not work at all.

* Pass out the Report Card and go over it with students. Explain that they should identify the parts of the text, give each part a grade, and make a comment. (You can adapt the Report Card to fit the text you've assigned and the elements you want students to focus on.)

* Create a Comment Sheet like the one shown below for the students to use as a reference.

* Discuss the grades that students gave as a whole class or ask small groups to do so. Challenge the class to try to reach a consensus on an overall rating for the text.

COMMENT SHEET

Illogical/confusing reasoning	Logical reasoning
Idea not clear	Sufficient reasoning
Wording is confusing.	Effective variety of reasoning
Evidence not convincing	Sentence(s) are clear.
Reasoning not sufficient to support claim	Good use of statistics
Poor vocabulary	Interesting, surprising vocabulary
Not enough sentence variation	Good sentence variation
No attention-grabber	Strong attention-grabber

Report Card

Reviewer: _____ Date _____

Author: _____ Title: _____

Grading Code:

E = Excellent   **S** = Satisfactory   **B** = Basic, Barely Acceptable   **U** = Unsatisfactory

"Subject" (Paraphrase or quote each)	Grade	Comment
1. Main Idea:		
2. Reason #1:		
2a. Evidence for Reason #1:		
3. Reason #2:		
3a. Evidence for Reason #2:		
4. Reason #3:		
4a. Evidence for Reason #3:		
5. Introduction and Conclusion Techniques: Label and explain.		
6. Word Choice and Style: Describe.		
7. Organization/Paragraphs		

Create an Ad

What It Is: An advertisement based on a persuasive text *(after reading)*

Use It With: Persuasive nonfiction

After reading a persuasive piece, students convert the author's argument and reasoning into a video, audio, or print advertisement. Whether students agree with the author or not, creating an ad will help them deeply explore the author's point of view. By the end of the assignment, students will have fully examined and evaluated the text and be poised to engage in a rich discussion of the issue raised by the author.

MATERIALS

✓ Assignment: Create an Ad for each student, p. 116

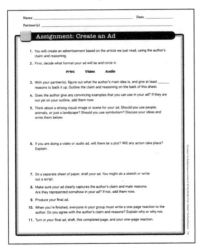

✓ A variety of video, audio, and print advertisements

✓ Posterboard, markers, crayons

✓ Sheets of paper

✓ Audio and/or video equipment for recording and playing ads (optional)

DIRECTIONS

* Have students work in groups. These could be smaller groups for print ads and larger groups for audio or video ads. All the groups can work on the same persuasive text, or you can assign a different text to each group.

* Introduce the assignment to students: *You will transform this text into a radio or television commercial or a newspaper or magazine ad. In your ad, the author's point of view should be prominent, and the reasoning should be clear. You must work with the author's claim, even if you don't agree with it—you'll have a chance to voice your own opinions at the end of the ad. Now, let's look at some examples of print and nonprint ads.*

  Then play and/or display the sample ads you've collected.

* Have students begin by outlining the author's claim and reasoning. Assign a minimum number of the author's reasons to include in their ads. Remind them to scan the text again for any examples that would be helpful to include in their ads.

* Students should discuss any visuals or scenes that would be effective in the ads. Should they use people, animals, or just a landscape? Should they use symbolism? If students are doing an audio or a visual ad, should there be a plot?

* Have students draft and create the ad.

* When their ads are finished, students should write a reaction to the author's claim and explain why they feel that way on a separate sheet of paper. Have them turn in their ad with the draft, and this one-page reaction.

* Hold a viewing of the ads. Discuss students' successful rendering of the author's claims and their own reactions to those claims.

BUILD A RUBRIC

Process: Brainstorming, planning, final product
Author's claim apparent in ad
Author's reasoning apparent in ad
Persuasiveness of ad (images, scene, plot)
Written reaction to author's claim
Effort, creativity

Name _____ Date _____

Partner(s) _____

Assignment: Create an Ad

1. You will create an advertisement based on the article we just read, using the author's claim and reasoning.

2. First, decide what format your ad will be and circle it:

   Print   **Video**   **Audio**

3. With your partner(s), figure out what the author's main idea is, and give at least _____ reasons to back it up. Outline the claim and reasoning on the back of this sheet.

4. Does the author give any convincing examples that you can use in your ad? If they are not yet on your outline, add them now.

5. Think about a strong visual image or scene for your ad. Should you use people, animals, or just a landscape? Should you use symbolism? Discuss your ideas and write them below:

6. If you are doing a video or audio ad, will there be a plot? Will any action take place? Explain:

7. On a separate sheet of paper, draft your ad. You might do a sketch or write out a script.

8. Make sure your ad clearly captures the author's claim and main reasons. Are they represented somehow in your ad? If not, add them now.

9. Produce your final ad.

10. When you're finished, everyone in your group must write a one-page reaction to the author. Do you agree with the author's claim and reasons? Explain why or why not.

11. Turn in your final ad, draft, this completed page, and your one-page reaction.

Human Likert Scale

What It Is: A physical activity in which students can show their reactions to an author's claims *(after reading)*

Use It With: Persuasive nonfiction

This fun and quick whole-class activity gets kids out of their seats and engaged! A Likert Scale, of course, is the popular rating-style questionnaire that requires the participant to answer each question with a number between, for example, one through five. The numbers can represent different feelings, but the most common system uses the high number to represent "Strongly Agree" and the low number to represent "Strongly Disagree." A Human Likert Scale, then, is not done on paper but in the front of a room; students can arrange themselves under giant numbers to show their feelings on a topic— in this case, an author's claim.

MATERIALS

✓ Five index cards for each pair

DIRECTIONS

* Have students read a persuasive article, noting the author's claim and reasons, and discuss it with a partner. Together, pairs should agree on the main thesis, supporting reasons, and examples the author uses in the text.

* Give each pair five index cards. On each card, partners should write an opinion; you specify the sources. For example, tell students that on three of the cards, they must write an opinion that is either directly stated in the article or that they inferred from the author's reasoning. For each opinion, they should reference a paragraph number from the text. On the final two cards, partners should come

CC CONNECTION!

By writing opinions on index cards and then choosing a reaction to each opinion, students will "delineate and evaluate the argument in a text" (R.8).

up with opinions related to the article's topic but not discussed in the article. These can include their own personal feelings about the topic. Point out to students that, on all cards, the opinions should take the form of statements, such as "Teens should be able to work at age 14" or "Cars should have a mechanism that automatically deactivates cell phone service when they start."

* While students are working on their index-card statements, write the numbers 1 through 5 across your board, allowing generous space between them. Under 1 write "Strongly Disagree" and under 5 write "Strongly Agree."

* When pairs have completed their index-card statements, collect all cards. (If you want to grade students for this, have them put their name on the back of each card.)

* Explain to the class the meaning and purpose of a Likert Scale. Describe how a Likert Scale is often used to survey people about their feelings on a certain topic, and how participants must rate their feelings between a range of numbers, such as between one and five. Most likely, students will already be familiar with this type of assessment, though they may not know its official name.

* Shuffle the cards, and ask students to stand in front of their seats. Read the first card. Students should arrange themselves along

the scale on the board according to how they feel about the stated opinion. You may want to write notes on the cards for later discussion with students.

* Continue through the cards, skipping repeats and noting interesting trends.

* Then have students sit and conduct a whole-class discussion. Some questions might include:

What was the author's main idea? Did most of the class agree or not?

Why would most of our class agree/disagree with the author (or be split, if that was the case)?

Which class arrangements surprised you? Why?

Which didn't surprise you?

Were any of the opinions difficult to choose a side about? Which ones?

Why do you think so many companies and groups use Likert Scales in their research?

 50 Common Core Reading Response Activities © 2014 by Marilyn Pryle, Scholastic Teaching Resources

Text Comparison Charts

What It Is: Handouts to help students compare and contrast different texts *(after reading)*

Use It With: Fiction and nonfiction

Over the course of the year, students should be able to compare what they're reading with other texts. To help students with this, you can have them examine themes across several texts, analyze the historical accuracy of a text, and identify connections and archetypes within a text.

MATERIALS

✓ Text Comparison Charts: Compare the Texts!, p. 120; Reality Check!, p. 121; Déjà Vu!, p. 122 for each student

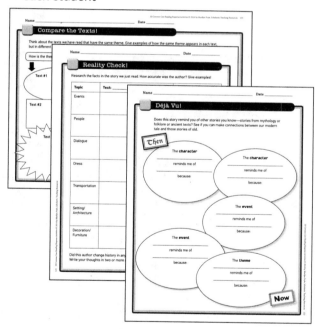

* First, students can look at different genres that center around a particular theme. Many districts are already doing this by setting up thematic units as their curriculum. A theme like "growing up" might involve a novel, a nonfiction narrative essay, a poetry sequence, and a science-fiction short story.

* Another way students can compare literature is to look into the historical accuracy of a piece of historical fiction by checking the author's facts and research, and asking themselves how authors use history, or even change it, when writing fiction.

* Finally, students can examine the archetypes in the modern stories they read—the characters or event sequences that remind them of ancient stories from various mythologies and traditional tales.

Notes on the Charts: Students will have to fill in the names of the texts (or you can do so before you copy the charts).

On the Compare the Texts! chart, you have the choice of assigning a theme or letting students decide on a theme themselves and writing it in the star.

On the Reality Check! chart, students' best bet for finding information is on the Internet. This is not included in the directions on the chart in case you have another source in mind. For an extra challenge on this chart, have students give quotes and page numbers from the text. The writing assignment at the bottom of this chart can be done with a partner or individually and used as a springboard for discussion.

On the Déjà Vu! chart, students should try to think of ways that characters and events and even themes can be found in stories of old, and fill in the stepping stones with examples.

Name _____ Date _____

Compare the Texts!

Think about the texts we have read that have the same theme. Give examples of how the same theme appears in each text, but in different ways.

How is the theme shown in each text?

How is that same theme a bit different in each text?

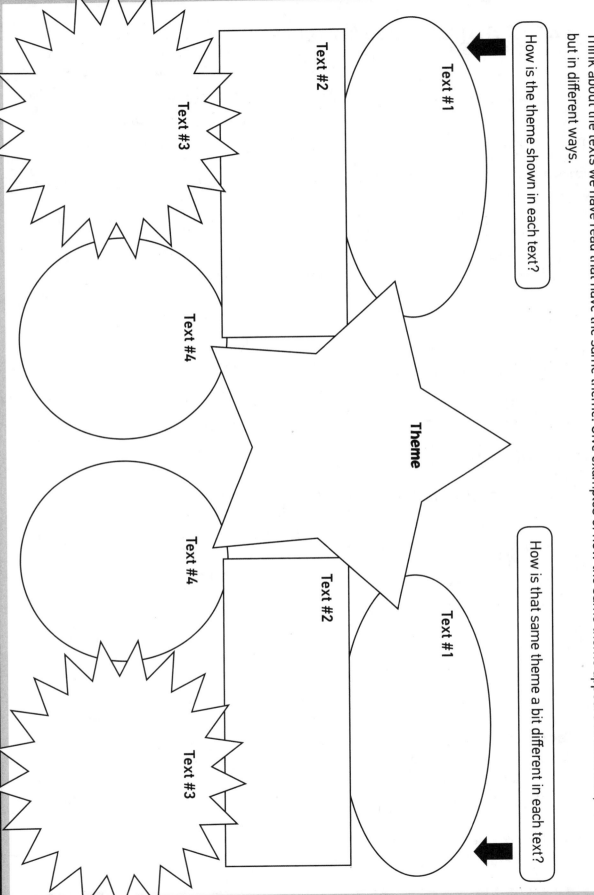

Text #1

Text #2

Text #3

Text #4

Theme

Text #4

Text #2

Text #1

Text #3

Reality Check!

Research the facts in the story we just read. How accurate was the author? Give examples!

Topic	Text: _____	Reality
Events		
People		
Dialogue		
Dress		
Transportation		
Setting/ Architecture		
Decoration/ Furniture		

Did this author change history in any way? How? Why do you think the author chose to do so? Write your thoughts in two or more paragraphs on the back of this page.

50 Common Core Reading Response Activities © 2014 by Marilyn Pryle, Scholastic Teaching Resources

Déjà Vu!

Does this story remind you of other stories you know—stories from mythology or folklore or ancient texts? See if you can make connections between our modern tale and those stories of old.

Then

The **character**

_____

reminds me of

_____

because:

The **character**

_____

reminds me of

_____

because:

The **event**

_____

reminds me of

_____

because:

The **event**

_____

reminds me of

_____

because:

The **theme**

_____

reminds me of

_____

because:

Now

News Vs. Opinion

What It Is: A comparison of a news article and an opinion article on the same topic *(after reading)*

Use It With: Nonfiction

This easy idea involves some research on your part. Give students a news article and an opinion piece on the same topic, and have them compare the two. You'll most likely be able to find both in the print or digital copy of your local newspaper or through an Internet search.

MATERIALS

✓ News Vs. Opinion for each student, p. 124

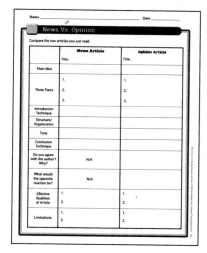

✓ Copy of news article

✓ Copy of opinion article

CC CONNECTION!

By directly comparing two articles of differing genres, students will "analyze how two or more texts address similar topics in order to compare the approaches the authors take" (R.9).

DIRECTIONS

* Find two articles on your topic: one news article and one opinion article. Let's say you want students to examine two articles about making the school day longer. You could do an Internet search on terms like "Opinion longer school day" and "News longer school day." Or, you could use a site like http://www.dailyoped.com to browse opinion articles, select one, and then search for a news article to match. You could focus on current events or topics that link to what you're reading, either historically or thematically.

* Give students the news article to read and annotate.

* Give students the opinion article to read and annotate.

* Have individuals or pairs complete the chart for the two articles, either separately or together, and then discuss the charts with the whole class.

News Vs. Opinion

Compare the two articles you just read.

	News Article Title:	Opinion Article Title:
Main Idea		
Three Facts	1. 2. 3.	1. 2. 3.
Introduction Technique		
Structure/ Organization		
Tone		
Conclusion Technique		
Do you agree with the author? Why?	N/A	
What would the opposite reaction be?	N/A	
Effective Qualities of Article	1. 2.	1. 2.
Limitations	1. 2.	1. 2.

Throw a Characters' Ball!

What It Is: A costume party during which students recite portions of text (*after reading*)

Use It With: Fiction and nonfiction

I've saved this activity for last because it works well at the end of the year, when students have read and absorbed most of the texts. Students love the build-up to the Characters' Ball, and this activity is easy for you to set up and grade.

MATERIALS

✓ Presentation: Character's Ball, p. 127

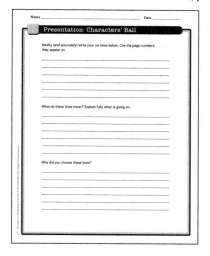

✓ Invitation to the Characters' Ball for each student

✓ A copy of the rubric on the next page for each student

✓ Clipboard

DIRECTIONS

* The success of the Characters' Ball will depend largely on your enthusiasm for it. Create and hand out official, fancy (but photocopied!) invitations about two weeks prior to the ball. Explain the premise: Students choose a character, an author, or some other symbol that relates to a piece of text they've read in class; they dress up

as that person or thing and recite six lines from the work. Assure students that they don't have to recite in front of the whole class—only to you as you walk around. But they must recap their understanding of those lines and explain why they chose that portion of text. Set a date for looking through texts and asking questions (usually a couple of days later).

* Allow time in class to search through texts for a six-line quotation. This in-class time is important, because a text may be back on the classroom shelf, the title of a sought-after poem forgotten, or the page number

Join the Fun!

To kick off the ball, have your own six lines memorized. Project the lines behind you as you recite—students will enjoy seeing you participate with them.

of a favorite passage "lost," and you can help students find what they're looking for.

* Pass out the Presentation: Characters' Ball sheet for students to complete. Copy the rubric at the bottom of the page on a separate sheet of paper, so they can see what they will be evaluated on. My rubric is shown below. (It's a bit more relaxed than the usual rubric.)

* Create an activity that students can complete during the Characters' Ball, such as asking them to visit every other student "character," identify his or her costume, and write a comment about it.

* On the day of the Character's Ball, explain the activity and instruct students to complete it while they mill about. As they socialize, visit each student individually. The student should hand you their completed Presentation: Characters' Ball sheet and then recite the lines on it. Give a grade on the spot, based on the rubric, and move on to the next student.

I realize that the Common Core does not require students to memorize text, but I believe there is great benefit to committing the words of established literature to heart. In addition, reciting text in a meaningful way—demonstrating an understanding of the words and their implications and using an appropriate tone— reinforces many of the standards. Besides, it's only a few lines. I tell students to choose the text and lines that *really* meant something to them during the year, from a character or an author they *really* cared about. This will ensure a greater level of understanding and investment.

The kids get into this, both with their costumes and the selection and delivery of their lines. If possible, make the Characters' Ball a real party with food, literary party favors that the kids can make beforehand, such as small, red, paper apples (from Lowry's *The Giver* [1993]) or cut-out Jolly Rogers (from Avi's *The True Confessions of Charlotte Doyle* [2012]), and decorations—but no music, as I've learned that it distracts students from the recitation of their lines. What a wonderful gift this is to send students away with at the end of the year—a fun memory, and lines of literature written in their hearts.

CHARACTERS' BALL RUBRIC

Costume: _____   Recitation: _____   TOTAL: _____

Costume		Recitation	
Great effort	(50)	Perfect	(50)
Good job	(40)	A couple of misses	(40)
Just all right	(30)	Half knew it	(30)
Not nothing	(20)	Knew a few words	(20)
None	(0)	Bagged it	(0)
BONUS: Completely Awesome! (+5)		**BONUS: Acted it out! (+5)**	

50 Common Core Reading Response Activities © 2014 by Marilyn Pryle, Scholastic Teaching Resources

Presentation: Characters' Ball

Neatly (and accurately) write your six lines below. Cite the page numbers they appear on.

_____

_____

_____

_____

_____

_____

What do these lines mean? Explain fully what is going on.

_____

_____

_____

_____

_____

_____

Why did you choose these lines?

_____

_____

_____

_____

_____

_____

50 Common Core Reading Response Activities © 2014 by Marilyn Pryle, Scholastic Teaching Resources

References

Alexie, S. (2007). *The absolutely true diary of a part-time Indian*. New York: Little, Brown and Co.

Anderson, L. H. (2000). *Fever 1793*. New York: Aladdin.

Anonymous. (1973). *Tales from the thousand and one nights* (N. J. Dawood, Trans.). London: Penguin Books.

Avi. (2012). *The true confessions of Charlotte Doyle*. New York: Scholastic.

Bacon, F. (1999). *The essays*. New York: Oxford University Press, Inc.

Bourdillon, F. W. [n.d.] Night. *All Poetry*. Retrieved from http://allpoetry.com/poem/8505533-The-Night-Has-A-Thousand-Eyes-by-Francis-William-Bourdillon

Brooks, G. (2005). We real cool. In *The essential Gwendolyn Brooks* (p. 60). New York: Literary Classics of the United States, Inc.

Cane, M. (1999). Snow toward evening. In B. Rogaski (Ed.), *Winter poems* (p. 16). New York: Scholastic, Inc.

Clifton, L. (1987). Sisters. In *Good woman* (p. 112). Brockport, NY: BOA Editions, Ltd.

Coffin, R. P. T. [n.d.] Secret heart. Retrieved from http://www.nexuslearning.net/books/Holt-EOL2/Collection%202/secretheart.htm

Creech, S. (1994). *Walk two moons*. New York: HarperCollins.

de la Mare, W. (2010). All but blind. In *down-adown-derry* (p. 64). New York: Henry Holt and Co.

Dickinson, E. (1960). I'm nobody! Who are you?. In *The complete poems of Emily Dickinson* (p. 288). Boston: Little, Brown and Co.

Elliot, T. S. (1968). Preludes. In *Collected poems, 1909-1962* (p. 13). New York: Harcourt, Brace and Co.

Fisher, A. (2007). Fall wind. In *Do rabbits have Christmas?*. New York: Henry Holt and Co.

Florian, D. (1999). Seashells. In X. J. Kennedy and D. M. Kennedy (Eds.), *Knock at a star* (p.136). Boston: Little, Brown and Co.

Francis, R. (1974.) Like ghosts of eagles. In *Like ghosts of eagles*. Amherst, MA: University of Massachusetts Press.

Frost, R. (1995). Bereft. In *Frost: Collected poems, prose and plays* (p. 230). New York: Literary Classics of the United States, Inc.

Frost, R. (1995). Nothing gold can stay. In *Frost: Collected poems, prose and plays* (p. 206). New York: Literary Classics of the United States, Inc.

Frost, R. (1995). The pasture. In *Frost: Collected poems, prose and plays* (p. 13). New York: Literary Classics of the United States, Inc.

Frost, R. (1995.) Stopping by woods on a snowy evening. In *Frost: Collected poems, prose and plays* (p. 207). New York: Literary Classics of the United States, Inc.

Gallagher, K. (2013, July 4). [Twitter post] https://twitter.com/KellyGToGo/status/352874878988337152

Green, R. L. (2008). *King Arthur and his knights of the round table*. London: Penguin Books.

Herford, O. (1966). Earth. In S. Dunning, E. Lueders, & H. Smith (Eds.), *Reflections on a gift of watermelon pickle* (p. 81). New York: Scott, Foresman and Co.

Hesse, K. (1997). *Out of the dust*. New York: Scholastic Inc.

Hinton, S. E. (2012). *The outsiders*. New York: Penguin Group, Inc.

Homer. (1998). *The Iliad*. (R. Fagles, Trans.). New York: Penguin Group, Inc.

Hughes, L. (1995). Dreams. In *The collected poems of Langston Hughes* (p. 32). New York: Vintage Books.

Hughes, L. (1995). Mother to son. In *The collected poems of Langston Hughes* (p. 30). New York: Vintage Books.

Hughes, L. (1995). Youth. In *The collected poems of Langston Hughes* (p. 39). New York: Vintage Books.

Hunter, K. (1995). The scribe. In D. Alvermann (Ed.), *Who's who?* (pp. 27–37). Lexington, MA: D. C. Heath & Co.

LeGuin, U. (1999). The child on the shore. In X. J. Kennedy and D. M. Kennedy (Eds.), *Knock at a star* (p. 54). Boston: Little, Brown and Co.

Levertov, D. (1966). The breathing. In *Poems of Denise Levertov, 1960–1967*. New York: New Directions Books.

Lewis, J. P. (2008, October 2). Stories. *Write Time*. Retrieved from http://lindakulp.blogspot.com/2008_10_01_archive.html

Lowry, L. (1993). *The giver*. New York: Random House.

Madgett, N. L. (1970). Woman with flower. In *Star by star*. Detroit, MI: Harlo Press.

Malam, C. (1984). Steam shovel. In J. Cole (Ed.), *A new treasury of children's poetry: Old favorites and new discoveries*. New York: Doubleday.

Merriam, E. (1992). Mean song. In *The singing green: New and selected poem for all seasons*. New York: HarperCollins.

Merriam, E. (1986). Metaphor. In *A sky full of poems*. New York: Yearling.

Merriam, E. [n.d]. Onomatopoeia. Retrieved from http://faculty.education.illinois.edu/j-levin/Davis/onomatopoeia.html

Milosz, C. (1990). Gift. In *The collected poems*. New York: Ecco.

Morrison, L. (1977). The sidewalk racer. In *The sidewalk racer and other poems of sports and motion*. New York: Lothrop, Lee & Shepard.

Oliver, M. (1992). Hawk. In *New and selected poems: Volume one* (pp. 34–35). Boston: Beacon Press.

Ovid. (1993). Daedalus and Icarus. In *The metamorphoses of Ovid*. (A. Mandelbaum, Trans.). Orlando, FL: Harcourt.

Poe, E. A. [n.d.] The raven. *Poetry Foundation*. http://www.poetryfoundation.org/poem/178713

Reeves, J. (1973). The sea. In *Complete poems for children*. London: Faber & Faber.

Riordan, R. (2005). *The lightning thief*. New York: Hyperion Books.

Riordan, R. (2006). *The sea of monsters*. New York: Hyperion Books.

Roethke, T. (1961). The waking. In *The collected poems of Theodore Roethke*. New York: Doubleday.

Rumi, Jalal ad Din. (1995). Elephant in the dark. In *The essential Rumi* (Coleman Barks, Trans.). New York: HarperCollins.

Sandburg, C. [n.d.] Fog. *The Poetry Foundation*. Retrieved from http://www.poetryfoundation.org/poem/174299

Sandburg, C. (1920). Summer stars. In *Smoke and steel* (p. 268). New York: Harcourt, Brace, and Howe.

Shakespeare, W. [n.d.] *The Tragedy of Julius Caesar*. Retrieved from *Open Source Shakespeare*, http://www.opensourceshakespeare.org/views/plays/playmenu.php?WorkID=juliuscaesar

Shortis, T. (2001). *The language of ICT*. London: Routledge.

Simic, C. (2000, March 6). Dog on a chain. *The New Yorker* (p. 58).

Steele, T. (1977). *Waiting for the storm*. Los Angeles: Horn Press.

Swenson, M. (2013). The universe. In Langdon Hammer (Ed.), *May Swenson: Collected poems*. New York: Library of America.

Updike, J. (1963). Sonic boom. In *Telephone poles and other poems*. New York: Knopf.

Whitman, W. [n.d.] When I heard the learn'd astronomer. *Poetry Foundation*. Retrieved from http://www.poetryfoundation.org/poem/174747

Williams, W. C. (1986). Poem (as the cat). In *The collected poems of William Carlos Williams: Vol. 1 1909–1939* (p. 352). New York: New Directions Press.